THE PERMANENT GUILLOTINE

Revolutionary Pocketbooks

THE PERMANENT GUILLOTINE
WRITINGS OF THE SANS-CULOTTES

Edited and translated by

Mitchell Abidor

The Permanent Guillotine: Writings of the Sans-Culottes
Edited and translated by Mitchell Abidor
This edition copyright © 2018 PM Press

ISBN: 978-1-62963-388-6
Library of Congress Control Number: 2016959609

Cover by John Yates/Stealworks
Layout by Jonathan Rowland based on work by briandesign

10 9 8 7 6 5 4 3 2 1

PM Press
PO Box 23912
Oakland, CA 94623
www.pmpress.org

Printed in the USA

■ CONTENTS

■ INTRODUCTION

When the Bastille was stormed and taken on July 14, 1789, it wasn't a crowd of breeches-wearing professionals that marched through the streets, attacked the prison, freed the internees, and killed its superintendent, carrying off his head on a pike. It was the working people of Paris, men who didn't wear breeches, the sans-culottes, who carried this out.

Two years later, on July 17, 1791, when the king was captured attempting to flee France and join his kindred in neighboring countries to make war on the revolutionary state, when the moderates of the Revolution were quite content to allow the king to maintain a defanged role in French life, it was these same sans-culottes who gathered on the Champ de Mars to demand the founding of a republic and who were brutally shot down.

A year later, with their revolutionary Fatherland in danger, again the sans-culottes went into action, emptying the prisons of Paris of enemies of their new republic, massacring imprisoned priests who had refused to swear loyalty to the republic, and setting up popular tribunals that resulted in a spontaneous Terror that led to the deaths of 1,100 foes. As a participant in these acts later wrote, "While we shuddered with horror at what was being done, we nevertheless realized that the massacres were inspired by the dictates of justice."

When just weeks later the time had come to carry revolutionary war to the enemy and the government called for volunteers, within a single week fifteen thousand men, almost all sans-culottes, answered the call, and at the Battle of Valmy they defeated the leagued forces of the émigrés, Prussia, Austria, and Hesse. As Albert Soboul wrote in his majestic history of the Revolution: "Against a professional army composed of highly disciplined men who passively obeyed the orders they received, the new army, national and popular in spirit, had fought and emerged victorious." And as Goethe, who was at the battle, said in one of his conversations with Eckermann: "This day and place open a new era in world history." And indeed, on September 21, 1792, the day the news of the victory reached the National Convention, royalty was abolished and the French Republic was proclaimed.

And then a year later, in 1793, when the campaign of dechristianization was launched, it was again the sans-culottes who pushed it hardest. The campaign, which began with the establishing of the republican calendar, replacing the existing one with a more "rational" division of time, including a ten-day week, and replacing the former names of months with names related to nature, had started out cautiously when it was directed from above. Cemeteries were secularized and carrying out any religious functions outside churches was banned. And then the sans-culottes, particularly the outspoken and profane Jacques Hébert, through the voice of his paper *Le Père Duchesne*, joined the campaign, and it took off in earnest. The cult of revolutionary martyrs replaced that of Christian martyrs; the bishop of Paris was forced to resign; and on November 10, 1793, a Festival of Liberty and Reason was held at Notre Dame Cathedral, complete with a mountain constructed in the church (symbolizing the Jacobins and the left), and the church itself was reconsecrated to the Cult of Reason. How far to the left the sans-culottes were became clear when they demanded that the state cease paying the salaries of priests: Robespierre and the Jacobins opposed the measure, fearing it would alienate neutral nations. The Jacobin government's success in slowing the pace of dechristianization was a pyrrhic one: it was the first clear sign of the Jacobin's fear of the sans-culottes, and halting dechristianization was the opening salvo in crushing the sans-culottes as an independent revolutionary force. The disappearance of this revolutionary wing ultimately left the Jacobins with no allies when they in turn were crushed on 9 Thermidor—July 27, 1794.

As Albert Soboul said of them in his study, *The Sans-Culottes*: "The Revolution was to a large extent their making. From the spring of 1789 to the spring of 1795, from the fourteenth of July to Prairial, Year III, they consecrated their energy to it. They placed all their hopes in it. They lived and suffered for it."

Who, then, were these sans-culottes, and what did they want of the Revolution they so loved?

It would be a serious mistake to view them as the working class. Though they were the precursors of the working class, in the conditions of late eighteenth-century France no such class truly existed. They were not factory workers, for there were no factories. They were a disparate group of small merchants, independent artisans, and hired laborers who had many desires in common, but not all, and so their demands, when they made them, reflected this multiplicity of points of view. However idealist and imprecise it might sound, the name given them by Jules Michelet, the greatest of French historians, might be the one that best characterizes them: "the people."

Standing against them was "the aristocracy," and just as "the people" can mean many things, so can "the aristocracy." For the sans-culottes anyone "respectable" was an aristocrat. They hated the aristocrats even for their attire: the clothing you wore expressed your political attitude (thus the king's popularity the day he donned the *bonnet phrygien*, the Liberty Bonnet that symbolized the Revolution) and to be decked out in finery was to be suspect. To wear fine clothing, to wear breeches, meant you were one of those who charged extortionate rents; who hoarded goods, thus raising their prices; who looked down of the people and their needs; who supported the king. So strong was this hatred of the respectable that in Year III, at the meeting of a revolutionary section, a woman called for the guillotining of every single "respectable person."

The positive sans-culotte demands did not include a socialist France, and when later historians like Daniel Guérin criticize their spokesmen for failing to establish a revolutionary vanguard party that would have led them to a socialist paradise, their criticism is revelatory of their lack of historical perspective and of an exacerbated case of anachronism. The sans-culottes were the most revolutionary section of the populace, insisting on the total dismantling and physical destruction of much of the old ruling class—the permanent guillotine was their ideal of justice—and though some of their demands do indeed have a socialist tinge, that is really the most that can be said for them. They wanted price controls put in place and maximum prices set for subsistence goods. They didn't want to abolish private property, but rather wanted restrictions on the amount that could be owned: they were merchants themselves and had no interest in seeing their livelihoods nationalized. In fact, as we see below in "The Sans-Culotte Alphabet," they don't want to take property for the simple reason that "I wouldn't want anyone to take mine." What they wanted was for there to be equality, absolute equality, believing that anything owned beyond the necessary was a superfluity. Their enemies were profiteers and hoarders, those who had any ties to the ancien régime, and those who provided goods of different quality to the wealthy and to the people. But it must be said again: the sans-culottes were not a class. Most of them were either artisans who made their living by the sweat of their brows or merchants of varying degrees of wealth and success. Expecting people with these varied interests to advance down the road to socialism is thus foolhardy, and to condemn them for failing to attain it unjust.

As "The Sans-Culotte Alphabet" demonstrates, they often considered themselves not an independent force, but rather the most militant supporters of the Jacobins, striving to keep that group on the revolutionary straight and narrow, though they were also strong in the Cordeliers Club. Robespierre and the Jacobins, skillful politicians that they were, made use of elements of the sans-culotte program to keep them within the fold, most importantly in the imposition of the "maximum," and as we have seen allowed them a certain amount of freedom, but not total freedom, in the dechristianization campaign. When any of their demands became too radical, or they posed a threat to the Jacobins and thus, in the eyes of the latter, to the Revolution itself, they were brutally brought back into line. More particularly, it was their leaders who were brought back into line and eventually guillotined.

Whatever the strength of the spontaneous outbursts of the masses, and however important the revolutionary sections were in giving vent to the ideas and sentiments of the sans-culottes, there nevertheless arose among them, or, more precisely, there went among them men who served as the primary voices of this diffuse mass.

Most important was Jacques Hébert, best known for his newspaper, written in the persona of the furnace maker Père Duchesne, who spoke the invective-filled French of the sans-culottes (though Hébert himself was the son of a bourgeois and called for the most extreme measures against the enemies of the Revolution: guillotining of the aristocracy, revolutionary war until victory, and insistence that the only way to ensure that profiteers weren't hoarding goods after the imposition of the maximum was executions and the use of the army for requisitioning).

These ideas ultimately led him to become a ferocious enemy of the Jacobins, whom he considered tepid and unwilling to see to it that profiteers were punished, and in March 1794, Hébert and his followers planned an uprising. Robespierre and his allies on the Committee of Public Safety, learning of the Hébertist plans, struck first, arrested him and his followers, placed him on trial on March 24, and that very evening Hébert and his followers were executed. Even the Jacobins realized the importance of this trial and execution in the revolutionary process: Saint-Just would say, "The Revolution is frozen."

Executed with Hébert was Anacharsis (né Jean-Baptiste) Cloots, the son of a wealthy Dutch family established in Germany, a man so Francophile that even before the Revolution he advocated the annexation of the left bank of the Rhine to France. With Cloots is born revolutionary internationalism, and he had two main focuses: spreading the French Revolution to the rest of Europe and a militant atheism far beyond the deism of Robespierre and his colleagues. So strong was his belief in himself and the universality of the ideals of the French Revolution that he assumed the title of "Orator of Humanity" and published newspaper called *The Universal Orator*. He would pay dearly for both his internationalism and his atheism: arrested by the Jacobins the same day as Thomas Paine, though not an intimate of Hébert, he was joined to the Hébertists at their trial and guillotined.

More controversial and a man "more difficult to grasp," in the words of the historian Albert Mathiez, was Jacques Roux, author of the key programmatic statement, "Manifesto of the Enragés." Roux was condemned during his lifetime by almost all who one would have supposed would be his allies, most particularly by Marat, whose assassination Roux was suspected of being involved in, and Jacques Hébert. Despite having been suspected of a role in Marat's death, so strong was his identification with the murdered "Friend of the People" that his newspaper (several selections from which are included in this collection) was entitled *The Publicist of the French Republic by the Shade of Marat*. This author of the essential text of the left of the French Revolution was considered by Mathiez to be "deceitful and ambiguous, seek[ing] in revolutionary preaching something other than the satisfying of his conscience."

Roux bragged of being among the first priests to swear allegiance to the Civil Constitution of the Clergy. And it was in his role of juring priest that he accompanied Louis XVI to the guillotine, leaving an account of the king's final moments. He far outdistanced in verbal extremism all around him, calling in a speech given in 1792 for the execution of all hoarders. It was his "Manifesto," though, with its calls for the strict application of the maximum and for the defense of the rights and lives of the sans-culottes that won him a popular following. But his extremism left him open to accusations of being an enemy of the Revolution, in fact a counterrevolutionary, and after a campaign was launched against him on precisely that count he was arrested in September 1793. Before he could be executed, he committed suicide in his cell. For posterity he remains the symbol of revolutionary intransigence: he appears as the strait-jacket-bound extremist madman in Peter Weiss's play *Marat/Sade*.

Not all of the figures of the left met this fate: Jean-François Varlet, along with Roux the key figure of those called the Enragés, was arrested with Hébert but survived that arrest, as well as another following the 9 Thermidor, living until 1837. Sylvain Maréchal, who had preceded and inspired the revolutionary government by devising a calendar that removed religion and religious figures, replacing them with heroes of Reason, participated in 1796 in Babeuf's Conspiracy of Equals, writing their manifesto, one of the foundational texts of communism. Maréchal's primary aim, though, was undermining religion, the basis of the unjust society under which he lived, and he dedicated much of his life to the antireligious struggle.

As can be imagined, history and historians have judged the sans-culottes and their leading figures in a dizzying array of fashions. Albert Soboul, in his study of them and their movement, credits them with having "constituted a powerful weapon of revolutionary struggle and national defense" in the first couple of years of the Revolution, and then in 1793, of having "made possible the inauguration of the revolutionary government, thus defeating counterrevolution at home and the coalition abroad." In the longer run, their victory in the great year of 1793 had as its direct result the Terror, which not only destroyed the Revolution's political enemies but also destroyed the old socioeconomic system, opening the way for the Thermidorian reaction to the growth of industrial capitalism, which caused great change for the artisanal sans-culottes, with some falling into the new proletariat and others climbing into the ranks of the new industrial bourgeoisie.

Views of their politics and place in the history of revolution in general reflect as much the politics of the historian as that of the popular forces.

For Albert Mathiez, the great early twentieth-century historian and briefly a member of the Communist Party, it was the Jacobins who were the true party of the left and voice of the people. In his 1920 *Le Bolchévisme et le Jacobinisme* (Bolshevism and Jacobinism) he posited "close ties and a logical kinship" between the two movements and presented Robespierre and Lenin as the very types of revolutionary leaders, even in their apparent differences:

> Let it not be objected that Robespierre respected private property while Lenin denied it. The difference in time periods explains the differences in theories and solutions, but the basis of things remains identical. In any event, Lenin did not suppress property. His measures are every bit as opportunistic as those of the Montagnards. They respond to the same necessities. There is no difference in nature between them.

And the goals of the Jacobins and the Bolsheviks were exactly the same:

> Robespierre and Lenin demanded the abolition of the death penalty. Once in power they made the ultimate penalty a method of governing. They had demanded the freedom of the press and they suppressed opposition newspapers. In short, the ends justify the means and absolve all contradictions. In both cases the end is the happiness of the masses.

Mathiez's view of the sans-culotte left of the Revolution was sympathetic, but far less than his support of Jacobinism:

he criticized their impatience as risking alienating neutrals like Switzerland and the United States, which explained and justified their being crushed. He nevertheless defends them: "Before becoming a danger they were a force. They were neither mad nor demented." Faint praise but praise nonetheless.

Daniel Guérin, in his influential ultra-left history of the Revolution, *Class Struggle in the First Republic*, on the other hand, dismisses the Jacobins as the voice of the interests of the bourgeoisie, men who had nothing but contempt for the sans-culottes. According to Guérin, Robespierre "did not like them, he was afraid of them," and he barely credits them with any revolutionary standing. Though he admires the Enragés' social program, his dogmatism leads him to condemn them for being "unable to take their thought to its conclusion. They could not link their economic demands to an ultimate objective which would transcend the confines of the existing system; nor indeed could they direct the mass movement toward a new form of power," as if the overthrow of a centuries-old autocracy, the execution of its leading figures, and the establishment of a republic in the space of less than four years was a minor advance. Essentially he condemns them for not having been able to transport France fifty years into the future, when there was a working class and the basis for a socialist society, or even more, almost a century and a quarter into the future so they could be proper revolutionaries. His utter ignorance of sans-culotterie is revealed in his condemnation of Hébert, along with Marat and Robespierre, as "passionate defenders of private property," as if the sans-culottes themselves were demanding the nationalization of production. What the sans-culottes, Hébert, Marat, and even the Jacobins (co-opting the left) put forth was as radical a program as was possible at the time. That it wasn't as radical as the most radical programs 150 years later is no grounds for criticism of them. As we have seen, they were themselves small property holders, and their interest was in limiting inequality, not in abolishing private holdings.

The anarchist Kropotkin, in his history of the Revolution, has nothing but praise for the sans-culottes and the Enragés, whom he considers the anarchists of the Revolution, whose ideas "later inspired Fourier, Godwin, Robert Owen, Proudhon, and their subsequent socialist fellows." If Guérin thought they lacked a vision of a new society, for Kropotkin "they saw that so long as commercial exploitation existed, nothing would be done; they maintained that to prevent this commerce would have to be communalized." Indeed, for Kropotkin, so strong was the influence of "the anarchists" that he credits the "armies of the sans-culottes [with] having enfranchised the peoples of Spain, Italy, Switzerland, Germany and Austria" under the leadership of Napoleon, the "ex-sans-culotte, now a general of the sans-culottes." If Guérin erred pessimistically in his anachronistic evaluation of the sans-culottes, Kropotkin errs optimistically in his anachronism.

The experience of the sans-culottes demonstrates the historical limits of their moment. They were the first popular moment to assault the heavens, to attempt a radical remaking of society. They pushed the French Revolution as far as the circumstances allowed. They were the main actors in the first act of the history of working-class revolution. They inspired all who came in their wake.

A SANS-CULOTTE MISCELLANEA

■ THE PERMANENT GUILLOTINE

(popular song of the sans-culottes)

Deputy Guillotin
In medicine
Quite expert and quite clever,
Made a machine.
To purge the French body
Of all those who plot.
It's the guillotine, ohé!
It's the guillotine!

To punish treason,
And high rapine,
Those lovers of coats of arms
Those people, you can guess who:
Those are who we made it for,
Those whose effect we know.
It's the guillotine, ohé!
It's the guillotine!

From having plotted,
That mutinous horde
Unexpectedly came down with
A bad headache.
One day,

In order to cure these gentlemen
We'll lead them
To the guillotine, ohé!
To the guillotine!

From France we've chased
The noble vermin,
We've swept crushed and,
Reduced everything to ruin,
But we've saved the nobleman
So as to kill him with a cut of the neck
By the guillotine, ohé!
By the guillotine.

Messieurs the noble mutineers,
Every one of whom vainly strives,
To foment civil war;

If we take you truly
You'll die very nobly.
On the guillotine, ohé!
On the guillotine.

The tenth[1] procured us
A hearty task,
The traitors abounded,
Worse than a plague.
Since we don't want to miss any
We punish without uprooting it.
Yes, the machine remains, ohé!
The machine remains.

---

1   The 10 Brumaire, Year II, date of the execution of the Girondins.

■ THE SANS-CULOTTE ALPHABET; OR, THE FIRST ELEMENTS OF REPUBLICAN EDUCATION

Dedicated to the Young Sans-Culottes
In their hearts new and pure, opening to life,
Let us engrave in strokes of fire the love of the
Fatherland.

I

Q: Who are you?
A: *A Republican*
Q: Who do you belong to?
A: *The Fatherland*

II

Q: What should you adore?
A: *The Supreme Being.*
Q: Through which sect?
A: *You are free to choose.*
Q: Which is preferable?
A: *That of nature and reason.*
Q: Tell me what this sect is.
A: *It's that which unites us with the Supreme Being or separates us from it.*

Q: How does it unite us?

A: *Through virtue.*

Q: How are we separated from it?

A: *Through crime.*

Q: Why should this sect be preferred?

A: *Because it is free of any superstition.*

Q: How does one recognize superstition?

A: *By its exaggerated dogmas, which tend to arm citizens the one against the other.*

Q: Does this sect consist of vain ceremonies?

A: *No.*

Q: Then in what?

A: *In pure morals, which will make humanity a people of brothers.*

III. On Morality

Q: What is the primary duty of a republican?

A: *That of being immutably and invincibly fixed on the good.*

Q: Why?

A: *Because this principle ensures his eternal happiness.*

Q: What is the most essential duty of a republican?

A: *That of submitting to the laws of his Fatherland.*

Q: What should a republican most frequently discuss?

A: *Justice, and for it alone he should work.*

Q: What difference is there between men?

A: *That of crime and virtue.*

Q: What is the most useful estate?

A: *That of the agriculturalist.*

Q: Why?

A: *Because he nourishes the others.*

Q: What is a republican's distinction?

A: *Merit.*

Q: His reward?

A: *Glory.*

Q: Define glory.

A: *It is reputation conjoined with esteem.*

Q: What are the sentiments innate to the soul of a republican?

A: *The love of liberty and equality and the hatred of tyrants.*

Q: What is the term of these sentiments?

A: *Death.*

Q: What is a tyrant?

A: *It is a man who through violence or ruse was able to expropriate the people's sovereignty.*

Q: *What should you honor?*

A: *Old age and those to whom I owe my birth.*

Q: How should you honor those to whom you owe your birth?

A: *By profiting from their instruction.*

Q: What are the greatest and first of all virtues?

A: *The love of the Fatherland and of humanity.*

Q: The most satisfying?

A: *Hospitality.*

Q: Whom should you assist?

A: *All the unfortunate.*

Q: Should you forget insults?

A: *Yes.*

Q: And good deeds?

A: *Never.*

Q: Can you take the property of others?

A: *No.*

Q: Why?

A: *Because I wouldn't want anyone to take mine.*

Q: What are the distinctive qualities of a republican?

A: *A great and strong soul. And this grandeur and strength should never lead him to make much of himself, but rather to vanquish himself, to commit no base deeds.*

Q: What does the honor of a republican consist of?

A: *Of never being frightened of any danger, of not retreating before any labor when it is useful to the Fatherland.*

Q: How should a republican be raised?

A: *In great sobriety, in the study of justice and war, in the exercise of all social and patriotic virtues, in great horror of all vices, especially that of ingratitude, and in great emulation for glory.*

Q: Why in great sobriety?

A: *Because sobriety preserves the health of the mind and the body.*

Q: Why in the study of justice?

A: *Because man's happiness derives from this study.*

Q: Why in that of war?

A: *In order to learn how to vanquish the enemies of the Fatherland.*

Q: Who are the enemies of the Fatherland?

A: *All tyrants.*

Q: Why should a republican be raised in this manner?

A: *Because his education is entirely directed toward public utility.*

Q: Can you hate anyone?

A: *Yes, the enemies of the Fatherland.*

Q: Can you take vengeance?

A: *No, the law alone has that right.*

Q: Is bearing false witness punished?

A: *Yes.*

Q: Why?

A: *Because the innocent must never be accused.*

Q: Should a republican allow himself to lie?

A: *No, he must always tell the truth.*

Q: Why is liberty so rare?

A: *Because it is the first of all goods.*

IV. On the Form of Government

Q: What is the form of government?

A: *Republican.*

Q: What does this word mean?

A: *A friend of the interests of all.*

Q: What is the government founded on?

A: *On justice.*

Q: What will support it?

A: *Enlightenment and independence, supported by force.*

Q: What is our constitution?

A: *Popular.*

Q: To whom do we owe this constitution?

A: *To the people and to that part of the Convention called the Mountain,[1] the true friends of the people.*

Q: What are the bases of this constitution?

A: *The rights of man, liberty, and equality.*

Q: Recite the rights of man.

A: *The French people, etc., etc.*

V. On the Division of Powers

Q: Of how many powers is the government composed?

A: *Two powers.*

Q: What are they?

A: *The legislative and the executive.*

Q: What is the legislative power?

A: *It's the National Convention, which makes the laws.*

Q: What is the executive power?

A: *It is the committees that execute them.*

VI. On the Division of the territory

Q: How do you divide the territory of the republic?

A: *Into departments.*

Q: And the departments?

---

1   The Jacobins, who sat at the top left of National Convention.

A: *Into districts.*

Q: And the districts?

A: *Into cantons.*

Q: And the cantons?

A: *Into communes.*

Q: Who renders justice?

A: *The judges.*

Q: Who names the judges?

A: *The people.*

Q: Who names to positions?

A: *The people.*

Q: Do the people also name to the National Assemblies?

A: *Yes, Citizen.*

Q: So everything is done by the people in the republic?

A: *Yes, Citizen.*

Q: Why?

A: *Because sovereignty resides in them alone.*

Q: Are all citizens subject to the laws?

A: *Yes, all equally.*

Q: So there is no individual in the republic who is inviolable?

A: *No. Only the people are inviolable.*

VII. Revolutionary History

Q: What are the most glorious dates of our Revolution?

A: *July 14, 1789, August 10, 1792, and May 31, June 1, and June 2, 1793.*

Q: What remarkable event occurred on July 14, 1789?

A: *The taking of the Bastille by the people of Paris.*

Q: Where was the Bastille?

A: *In Paris.*

Q: What was the Bastille?

A: *A horrible prison, where the tyrant buried alive those who dared raise their voices against the tyranny.*

Q: What happened on August 10, 1792?

A: *The attack on the tyrant's palace by the brave sans-culottes of the faubourgs, assisted by all their brothers of the departments, and their victory.*

Q: What did this victory produce?

A: *The fall of the tyranny and freedom.*

Q: What is a brave sans-culotte?

A: *It's a man whose soul can't be broken by the gold of despots.*

Q: What are the virtues of a sans-culotte?

A: *All of them.*

Q: What remarkable events happened May 31, June 1, and June 2, 1793?

A: *They were memorable days that complemented the preceding ones by destroying the conspirators, their liberticide plots, and ensuring the unity and indivisibility of the republic.*

Q: So these revolutionary days were necessary?

A: *Yes, for without them there would be no more liberty.*

Q: Is it necessary to prolong them?

A: *Yes, as long as tyranny lasts.*

Q: Who are the men who deserved well of the Fatherland?

A: *The men of July 14, 1789, those of August 10, 1792, and those of May 31, June 1, and June 2, 1793.*

Q: In what way did they deserve well of the Fatherland?

A: *By ensuring twenty-five million people freedom and equality.*

Q: Where will this freedom reach?

A: *The ends of the earth.*

Q: Who is it that most contributed to propagating it?

A: *The citizens who make up the society of Jacobins.*

Q: Who were the first martyrs to freedom?

A: *Two representatives of the people.*

Q: Name them.

A: *Pelletier and Marat, the Friend of the People.*

Q: Who assassinated them?

A: *Monsters animated by the royalists, priests, and federalists.*

Q: What will national vengeance be?

A: *The death of all tyrants.*

Q: What was done with their bodies?

A: *They were deposed in the Panthéon.*

Q: What is the Panthéon?

A: *It's a superb edifice destined to hold the ashes of those men who have deserved well of the Fatherland.*

Q: Was there another martyr for liberty?

A: *Yes.*

Q: Where?

A: *In Lyon, currently Ville Affranchie (Freed City).*

Q: Name him.

A: *Chalier, president of the tribunal of the district of Lyon.*[2]

Q: Who had him sacrificed?

A: *The counterrevolutionaries of that guilty commune.*

Q: Was he also given the honors of the Panthéon?

A: *Yes, for he died for liberty.*

Q: Who are those who will be called martyrs?

A: *Those who will die for liberty.*

Q: Name the ancients who loved liberty.

A: *Brutus, Mutius Scaevola, William Tell.*

Q: Who are the men who, through their writings, prepared the Revolution?

A: *Helvetius, Mably, J.-J. Rousseau, Voltaire, Franklin.*

Q: What do you call these great men?

A: *Philosophers.*

Q: What does this word mean?

A: *Wise man, friend of humanity.*

Q: What do their works teach?

A: *That we must adore the Supreme Being, be subject to his laws, and love men.*

---

2 Marie Joseph Chalier (1747–1793)—revolutionary leader, militant fighter against the moderates, murdered by them in Lyon.

Q: What else do they teach?

A: *The practice of all virtues, and that we must sacrifice what is most dear to us to the interests of the Fatherland.*

Q: What is our oriflamme?

A: *The tricolored flag.*

Q: What is our victory cry?

A: *Long Live the Republic! Long Live the Mountain!*

VIII. On the State of the Republic at the Beginning of the Campaign

Q: Where was the republic at the beginning of the campaign?

A: *In a few decrees, in the hearts of a small number of firm men, devoted to the death to rise up to liberty.*

Q: What was the state of our armies?

A: *They were naked, unfinished, and formed of recruitments made in the midst of a civil war.*

Q: By whom were they commanded?

A: *By traitors sold out to tyrants in coalition against France.*

Q: Who were the administrators of the departments?

A: *They were Brissotins, Rolandists,[3] royalists, and, to put it in one word, federalists.*

Q: Was the Convention better composed?

A: *We saw there both the wheat and the chaff, and incorruptible Montagnards destined for the dagger and slander.[4]*

Q: What was the situation in the southern part of the republic?

A: *It was threatened by a moral defection and a military invasion.*

---

3 Followers of Jacques Pierre Brissot (1754–1793) and Jean-Marie Roland (1734–1793)—leaders of the moderate Girondins. Both were guillotined

4 Montagnards: the Jacobins—the inhabitants of the Mountain, the highest seats in the chamber of the Convention.

Q: Was the north in a less disastrous position?

A: *No, it was betrayed and sold out to England and Austria, as was the Rhine.*

Q: Did the coastal borders share this sad lot?

A: *Yes, they were corrupted by the gold of English merchants.*

Q: What had become of the republican spirit?

A: *It was debased, tormented, denounced to federalist opinion.*

Q: What was the state of the public treasury?

A: *It was dried up, pillaged; the gold and silver had disappeared.*

Q: Didn't the state's minted money ease this exhaustion?

A: *No, the enemies of the republic had too debased it.*

Q: The constitution was thus without force and vigor?

A: *Alas, we didn't have any.*

Q: What is the Vendée that is so talked about?

A: *The lair of royalists, aristocrats, émigrés, fanatical priests, swindlers, and intriguers.*

Q: What did these wretches do there?

A: *Assisted by exhausted peasants, in concert with Pitt and Cobourg, they prepared the counterrevolution.*

Q: Was this country the only one that conspired against the republic?

A: *No. The commune of Lyon, that of Toulon, even Marseilles had changed camps.*

IX. On the Current State of the French Republic

Q: Where is the republic today?

A: *In the unwavering vows of its representatives, in the courage of the armies, in the will of the people, in the popular societies, in the victories in the Vendée, in Lyon and Marseilles, and in the hearts of the honest sans-culottes, freed of monarchical and religious prejudices and knowing nothing but the god of nature, of reason, and of liberty.*

Q: What is the present situation of the republic?

A: *It will soon achieve its great destiny.*

Q: What is the foundation on which it rests its hope?

A: *On a republican constitution, where sacred equality finds itself consecrated for the first time.*

Q: Do we have armies to make it respected?

A: *Yes, and twelve for one, all in full activity.*

Q: By whom are they commanded?

A: *By honest republicans, by true sans-culottes.*

Q: How was so immense a levee carried out?

A: *By a tiny decree of one line.*

Q: Was there not a second decree to reinforce these armies?

A: *Yes.*

Q: What did it produce?

A: *A levee of six hundred thousand men executed in the blink of an eye by a spontaneous movement.*

Q: When was it carried out?

A: *At a moment when we lacked supplies and arms.*

Q: So the Convention is quite powerful?

A: *Its power is limitless, for it has as its foundation the confidence and love of twenty-five million men.*

Q: Did it purge itself of the members who soiled its sanctuary?

A: *Most have already suffered the penalty due their misdeeds, and it daily delivers to the sword of the law all those whose perfidy is revealed.*

Q: Our representatives are thus no longer inviolable?

A: *No, they have been stripped of a prerogative useless to virtue and favorable to crime.*

Q: What effect was produced by the just punishment of deputies who dishonored their august character?

A: *It has recalled the Convention to its dignity, its unity, and the energy appropriate to the representatives of a democratic republic.*

Q: What is the state of the constituted authorities?

A: *They were scrupulously purged and assist in public happiness with everything that is within their power.*

Q: And that celebrated society, the cradle of liberty and equality and its strongest rampart, does it still have its energy and splendor?

A: *Yes. The sacred flame that consumed the soul of Aristide and Brutus can still be found at the Jacobin Club; it is there, on the Mountain, that the grateful Fatherland contemplates its most intrepid defenders.*

Q: What has become of royalism?

A: *It as destroyed or deported, along with the infamous race that might reproduce it.*

Q: And federalism?

A: *It died on the gallows.*

Q: What was the fate of the cities that revolted against the republic?

A: *Lyon was violently returned to its bosom.*

Q: And Toulon?

A: *It was taken in an assault against the English who had bought it off.*

Q: What became of its perfidious inhabitants?

A: *Most of those traitors were guillotined or shot. The rest carried the opprobrium that covered them to the enemy.*

Q: What is the state of the public treasury?

A: *It overflows with the immense riches of fanaticism, the treasures of traitors, conspirators, and émigrés.*

Q: And the assignats?

A: *They have recovered the value they never should have lost.*

Q: So new taxes weren't created?

A: *Not the smallest, though the republic spends 400 million per month.*

Q: What is our fundamental maxim?

A: *Unity and indivisibility.*

Q: What are our defense and our strength?

A: *Unity and indivisibility.*

Q: What is our salvation?

A: *Unity and indivisibility.*

Q: What is the goal we are headed toward?

A: *The peaceful enjoyment of liberty and equality; the reign of that eternal justice whose laws, as Robespierre so well said, are engraved in the hearts of all men, and even in those of the slave who forgets them and the tyrant who denies them.*

X. On the Situation of the Coalition of Kings

Q: What is the state of the armies of the kings in coalition against the republic?

A: *They are frightened, decomposed, and lacking in effectives.*

Q: Is it easy for the places to be filled?

A: *Oh, not at all. The allies can only obtain recruits and militias through threats, violence, and chains, or by forcing the residents of cities and dragging along those from the countryside.*

Q: What is the state of their finances?

A: *They have long since been exhausted.*

Q: How then can these tyrants meet the expenses of so ruinous a war?

A: *By contracting loans from wherever they can—having crushed their imbecilic subjects under the weight of taxes.*

Q: How, without funds and with troops that they force to fight, do they dare attempt to resist the enormous might of the French and their immense resources?

A: *Having learned from experience, they no longer hide the difficulty or, more accurately, the impossibility of doing so, but their pride prevents them from begging for the clemency of a magnanimous nation.*

Q: What will be the result of their united efforts?

A: *The overturning of their shaky thrones and the triumph of the universal liberty of nations.*

From *Alphabet des sans-culottes, ou premiers éléments de l'education républicaine.* Paris: G.-F. Gallet, Year II.

■ YOU WON'T THUMB YOUR NOSES AT US!

Address of the Brave Sans-Culottes to the National Convention delivered November 28, 1792

Legislators:

Feeling the sharpest of pain at the sight of the hatred and dissension that reign among you, the sans-culottes will in this place and with their usual energy condemn you for your slowness, your inexactitude, your inaction, and will prove to you that you are thumbing your noses at us.

You order us to make ourselves a constitution, to see to our needs, and to save the Fatherland. What do you do to fulfill your mission? It appears you possess all the means to ignite civil war and to propagate anarchy.

The whole of your sessions is spent in vain denunciations, in vain responses to denunciations. You eloquently tell us that Robespierre wants to be dictator. You incite public hatred against him. You carpet the streets of the capitol with posters on which you threaten this one and that one. Honestly, is this the sublime role that legislators should play? What does it matter to us that Robespierre wanted to be dictator; that he wanted to elevate Marat to that dignity? Don't you know that we said that we no longer want a master? You say that this Marat is a blood-thirsty man who constantly incites the people to murder and carnage. What a high opinion of the people you have! What? You think that Marat will incite the people to carnage? You're thumbing your noses at us.

Know that the people are just, and that when you all conspire together to command them to commit an injustice, they will know how to punish your daring.

Let us pass now to your decrees.

In the more than two months that you have been assembled, what have you done? You decreed the fall of the king. You metamorphosed the monarchy into a republic, and you have fulfilled our wishes. We hoped for tranquility and peace after this, and we thank the divinity for having so well enlightened us on the choice to be made; our happiness did not last long. We were suddenly seized with vertigo. The perfidious king should have been punished for his crime: this was the hope of all Frenchmen, and two months later you still haven't decided if he is to be judged.

You decreed that your sessions would begin at 9:00 and that you would spend two hours on the judgment of the king. And have you executed this decree? No, because at 11:00 there are never more than fifty deputies in the hall. Gentlemen, you should preach by example. An honorable member, who was probably bothered by having to get up so early, thus had it decreed—to your great contentment—that you would spend two sessions a week on this famous trial, and the previous decree fell by the wayside. You think you will lull us for a long while yet, but believe us: the people have seen that you are thumbing your noses at them.

You say that the constitution rendered him inviolable. Did we sanction this constitution? No, because we just abolished it. In vain you speak to us of other nations. We want, and we have always wanted, no one in the republic to be above the law. It would even be cruel not to judge him. The king is either guilty or innocent. In the latter case should you be keeping him in prison? On the contrary, shouldn't he, like you, enjoy the benefits of liberty and equality?

Aren't you thumbing your noses at us when you tell us that Paris and all of France are threatened with a famine and that we have to buy wheat from other countries? Do you think us foolish enough to believe that after as abundant a harvest as the last one we are forced to borrow from foreigners, as is almost always the case. But we know full well that the clique of profiteers have enormous storehouses in Jersey and elsewhere. But we also know that much more is left for us than we need. By a rigorous decree, force the large landowners, the big farmers, and all those who have storehouses of this basic commodity to take their wheat to the market. Tax the price of it in keeping with its differing qualities and put it in storehouses that will be under your discreet surveillance.

You will doubtless object that this goes against the system of liberty that you have established. On the contrary, we are going to prove that in not doing this you will forever annihilate liberty and equality. In fact, a hundred individuals who would hoard all the production of the empire could very easily put the nation again in the yoke by giving or refusing it food. Only that portion of men would then be free. You are certainly not ignorant of the fact that this was the infamous policy of the tyrants who, to have themselves loved by the people, as the need arose decreased the price of bread, which they did quite often before weighing them down with new irons, because, they said, the canaille no longer cries out when they have bread.

You are told that Paris only has provisions for a month, and you still don't act. Who did you charge with seeing to the subsistence of that great city? Bakers, wretches who, together with Necker, caused a frightful famine in 1789, the example of which has never been found in the history of any people.

Legislators, we repeat, it is time that you put an end to profiteering, that you rigorously punish its practitioners, for your negligence is beginning to make us believe that some among you are the chiefs or the accomplices in this infamous traffic. And when the people have suspicions, they almost always see their suspicions turn into reality.

We thought it our duty to warn you and advise you that we would hate to be forced to make the National Convention experience the same fate as the former municipality. We know the principal profiteers, and we will do them the kindness of not naming them here, persuaded that, having regained their senses at the sight of the misfortunes into which they would precipitate the republic, they will be the first to accept this demand.

If this petition doesn't meet with the success we have the right to expect, then we'll make a new one, which will be the last one, in which we will reveal all the traitors who, under the mask of patriotism, want to overturn the holy edifice of liberty and equality. And then we'll see if you'll still thumb your noses at us.

Paris, this 28th of November 1792
The first year of the Republic.

■ SECOND AND FINAL ADDRESS OF THE BRAVE SANS-CULOTTES

You won't long thumb your noses at us
All I did was blow on them and they were gone

The majesty of the people is degraded by your baseness. Your ruses and intrigues are no longer a mystery. Tremble, wretches: you have been unmasked!

In our first address we called on you to meet our demands. Far from having responded to our orders, you have the audacity to scorn them. Well then, we're going to speak the language of truth: in a week you'll no longer thumb your noses at us. While rendering justice to the patriotism, the wisdom, and the firmness of some of you, we will strike horribly those who dared compromise national dignity and betray the sacred interests of the people.

Rightly alarmed by the dangers confronting the republic, by the shortage of subsistence goods, we thought it our duty to show you in two words the sole method of remedying this. Did you carry this out? No! You even acted as if you weren't paying attention. Ten days ago, we told you that Paris was about to run out of subsistence goods. What did you do? You began long and vain discussions on the judging of the *ci-devant* king, which you are in no hurry to soon end. (One can see that you're not tired of receiving our twenty-one livres.) You received addresses, thanks, etc.; you formed the plan of a congratulatory address to the generals and soldiers of the Fatherland, who lack shoes, bread, and money; you engaged in denunciations of Mirabeau, who, if he were still alive, would cause you to tremble with a sole look; you revealed plans of conspiracies known by all, and this occupied three-quarters of your sessions—and yesterday Paris lacked bread. Finally, during long debates that lasted the three-quarters of your sessions you issued a decree calling for the death penalty against those opposed to the free circulation of grains. Do you think that through this decree you've remedied the famine? No, and you know this full well. Do you think we don't see that you are in the trade? For what good is it to decree the death penalty against those who oppose the free circulation of grains if you don't decree the same punishment against the profiteers, the landlords, the large famers who are involved in this infamous commerce?

So in two words we will explain to you the cause of the current famine and point out the guilty parties. The surrounding provinces are full of wheat, but who owns it? The big farmers, the big landlords, the financiers, and the ministers, or those who purchase in their name. The big farmers, aside from their harvest, purchase wheat under the pretext that they no longer have any available for their planting. The rich landlords do the same, and keep their wheat as straw for long periods without grinding it. They even purchase some for their own meals. At the same time, it is only small landowners and poor laborers who bring their wheat to the markets. Since they are forced to sell quickly in order to meet their needs their small stock, which is generally purchased by profiteers and placed in their warehouses, is soon exhausted. The people of the countryside have no money and can't purchase provisions, so they have started to bring little wheat to the market. The public is told that there is no more wheat in the country; that everything was taken to provision the army. These provisions are slightly increased and those who provide for Paris are forced to resort to this base canaille, who sell them whatever they want and who sell even more dearly to their own fellow citizens, still under the pretext that in doing so they deprive themselves and that they have none for their own consumption. After all this, legislators, why do you find it extraordinary that that the people in such a country, afraid of an imminent famine, oppose the removal of grain from their own soil? Under these circumstances tell me who should be punished, the people or those who misled while sucking the last drop of their blood?

I hear you all cry out: What is the remedy for these calamities? Most of you know. We already told you what it was: tax the price of wheat and the merchandise of primary necessity; force the rich landlords to bring their crops to the market; but above all, tax forever, and you'll see that without cracking down on them they'll be obliged to come to market because they'll expect no lucre from their intrigues. Yes, legislators, we order you to do this: tax bread and meat. You know that it is we who raised you up and that with a mere swipe of the hand we can bury you in the obscurity from which you would never have emerged without our order. Fulfill your mission or in a week you will no longer thumb your noses at us. We know we won't be listened to; we know that three-quarters of you are either landlords or farmers or the sons of that execrable mob. We confess that we were fooled, but after having ignominiously driven you out, you can be sure that such an error will serve us as a lesson.

Patriots of the Assembly, these reproaches are not addressed to you. We are fair. Nevertheless, you, virtuous Pétion,[1] who knows all these maneuvers as well as we do, why, instead of amusing yourself in having Mirabeau denounced,[2] weren't you the first to unmask these base intrigues that starve a people that testified to its esteem for you? Why do you seem to waver between the two parties that are currently dividing the Convention? And you, incorruptible Robespierre, Merlin,[3] and other patriots, who energetically fulfill the august role we confided you with, we warn you: you are the dupes of the enemies of the republic; they want to amuse you with false letters and false plots in order to delay the justly merited punishment of the most perfidious and cowardly of kings. They want to distract you from a law on subsistence goods because they hope that the people, lacking in everything, will be driven to excesses that might assist them in their criminal conspiracies. We know them, these conspiracies, and we will never cease to denounce them to you, as well as the traitors who want to madly thumb their noses at us. We will give you their names; we'll unmask all their base intrigues; we will cover their guilty heads with shame and contempt.

You brave sans-culottes of the eighty-three departments, unite with us! Together let us drive out that unholy horde that wants to attack our holy freedom and prove to the entire universe, by exterminating all these petty

---

1   Jérôme Pétion de Villeneuve (1756–1794)—important figure among the moderate Girondins. Declared an enemy of the republic, he fled and committed suicide before he could be captured.
2   Honoré Mirabeau (1749–1791)—orator, political thinker, and diplomat. Nicknamed "The Hercules of Liberty."
3   Merlin de Thionville (1762–1833)—member of the National Convention, expelled by the Jacobins. Representative on Mission with the armies in the Rhine, the Vosges, and the Moselle.

tyrants, that the sans-culottes know how to fight, win, and give themselves laws.

Yes, our brave friends, our representatives, are thumbing their noses at us. Let these wretches tremble! We have unmasked then, and since they want to destroy the Fatherland, we will prove to them that we will know how to save it. Don't get discouraged: ignominiously drive out these villains, and may their just punishment teach anyone tempted to imitate them that we will never suffer anyone thumbing his nose at us.

Paris, December 9, 1792
First Year of the French Republic

■ THE POPULAR SOCIETY OF SANS-CULOTTES OF NÎMES

to the National Convention
18 Messidor, Year II (July 6, 1794)

Legislators:

While we wait for the energy of the revolutionary government and the habit of revolutionary virtues to form vigorous souls capable of receiving the austere regime of Sparta, let us put to the test an important element of the political system that that famous republic adopted. When a child was born there he was taken from his parents in order to become more particularly a child of the Fatherland. He was immediately wrested from harmful preferences, limp caresses, and the dangerous antipathies of the family in order to be raised in the love and reciprocal duties of the great family that is the state. If it is ever important to imitate this great example of patriotism it is toward these children, whose habits, impressions, and prejudices must be reformed, and to renew, if possible, the blood transmitted in their veins. We are speaking of those children who have been rendered orphans through their parents' crimes, of those unfortunate offspring of a rotten branch that national justice tore from the soil of Liberty. Let us take hold of them and receive them in orphanages where they will be sheltered from any of the malignant influences, perfidious suggestions, and hatreds nourished in their souls by mothers who grew up in servitude, encrusted in prejudices, and perhaps full of a culpable resentment. Energetic supervisors should distribute to them, along with the bread of the Fatherland, the virile and austere lessons of republicanism. May these children be reborn and may liberty be the first thing they see. Hurry! Let their primary needs not provoke their complaints. Let your haste forestall the criminal sentiments that will not fail to be planted in their souls. Let them quickly suck a new milk capable of regenerating them and preserving them for the Fatherland, which will have done everything for them. This tender mother will inspire nothing but gentle affection in them; she will not sacrifice them to the ambitious fury of inequality or to the blind frenzy of barbarous prejudices.

Signed,
Pélissier, president
The secretaries: *Beaucourt, the eldest son*
              Colomb
              Rame
              Abot

JACQUES
ROUX
(1752–1794)

■ MANIFESTO OF THE ENRAGÉS

Address presented at the National Convention in the name of the Sections of Gravilliers, Bonne-Nouvelle and the Cordeliers Club by Jacques Roux

> People, I brave death to support your rights; prove to me your recognition by respecting persons and property.
> —Jacques Roux

Delegates of the French people!

One hundred times this hall has rung with the crimes of egoists and knaves; you have always promised to strike the bloodsuckers of the people. The constitutional act is going to be presented to the sovereign for sanction: Have you outlawed speculation there? No. Have you called for the death penalty against profiteers? No. Have you determined what freedom of commerce consists of? No. Have you forbidden the sale of minted money? No. Well then, we say to you that you haven't done everything for the happiness of the people.

Freedom is nothing but a vain phantom when one class of men can starve another with impunity. Equality is nothing but a vain phantom when the rich, through hoarding, exercise the right of life or death over their like. The republic is nothing but a vain phantom when the counterrevolution can operate every day through the price of commodities, which three-quarters of all citizens cannot afford without shedding tears.

Nevertheless, it's only by stopping the brigandage of trade, which must be distinguished from commerce; it's only by putting comestibles within the reach of the sansculottes that you will attach them to the Revolution and rally them around the constitutional laws.

And is it because unfaithful representatives, the statesmen, have called down on our unfortunate Fatherland the plague of foreign war that the rich should declare a more terrible one internally? Is it because three hundred thousand Frenchmen, traitorously sacrificed, perished by the homicidal steel of the slaves of kings that those who remained in their homes should be reduced to devouring stones? Is it necessary that the widows of those who died for the cause of freedom pay, at the price of gold, for the cotton they need to wipe away their tears, for the milk and the honey that serves as food for their children?

Representatives of the people, when you had among you the accomplices of Dumouriez,[1] the representatives of the Vendée, the royalists who wanted to save the tyrant; those execrable men who organized the civil war, those inquisitorial senators who viewed patriotism and virtue as crimes, the Gravilliers Section suspended its judgment. It saw that it wasn't within the power of the Mountain to do the good that was in its heart, it rose up. . . .

---

1   Charles-François Dumouriez (1739–1823)—general who led the revolutionary forces at Valmy. Attempted to overthrow the revolutionary government in 1793 and fled France.

But today, when the sanctuary of the laws is no longer soiled by the presence of Gorsas,[2] Brissot, Barbaroux,[3] and other chiefs of the those who called for the appeal to the people before executing the king; today when these traitors, in order to escape the gallows, have gone to hide their nullity and infamy in those departments they've whipped up against the republic; today when the National Convention has been returned to its dignity and vigor, and when in order to do good it need only want to do so, we call on you, in the name of the salvation of the republic, to strike speculation and profiteering with a constitutional anathema, and to decree the general principle that commerce doesn't consist in ruining, rendering hopeless, or starving citizens.

For the last four years only the wealthy profited from the Revolution. The mercantile aristocracy, more terrible than that of the noble and priestly aristocracy, has made a cruel game of invading individual fortunes and the treasury of the republic; we still don't know what will be the term of their exactions, for the price of merchandise rises frightfully from morning to evening. Citizen representatives, it is time that the combat unto death that the egoist carries out against the hardest working class of society come to an end. Pronounce against speculators and profiteers: either they'll obey your decrees or they won't. In the first hypothesis you will have saved the Fatherland; in the second case you will still have saved the Fatherland, for we will have been able to identify and strike the bloodsuckers of the people.

---

2   Antoine Joseph Gorsas (1752–1793)—journalist and member of the National Convention. A furious opponent of Robespierre and Danton. Guillotined.
3   Charles Jean Marie Barbaroux (1767–1794)—Girondin leader. Arrested as an enemy of the republic, he escaped, formed an army to fight the National Convention, was captured and guillotined.

And can the property of knaves be more sacred than the life of a man? Armed force is at the disposal of administrative bodies; how can they not be able to requisition those goods necessary to life? The legislator has the right to declare war, in other words to have men massacred. How could he then not have the right to prevent the grinding down and starvation of those who guard their homes?

The freedom of commerce is the right to use and to make use of, and not the right to tyrannize and prevent use. Those goods necessary to all should be delivered at a price accessible to all. Pronounce then. . . . The sans-culottes will execute your decrees with their pikes.

You didn't hesitate to strike with death those who would dare propose a king, and you did well; you have just outlawed those counterrevolutionaries in Marseilles who reddened the gallows with the blood of patriots, and you did well. You would have deserved well of the Fatherland if you would have put a price on the head of the fugitive Capets and the deputies who deserted their posts; if you would have expelled from our armies the nobles and those of the court who held their places; if you would have taken hostage the wives and children of émigrés and conspirators; if you would have held the pensions of the *ci-devant* privileged to pay the costs of the war; if you would have confiscated the treasures acquired since the Revolution by bankers and profiteers for the benefit of volunteers and widows; if you would have chased from the Convention the deputies who voted for the appeal to the people; if you would have turned over to revolutionary tribunals the administrators who provoked federalism; if you would have struck with the sword of justice the ministers and the members of the executive council who allowed a counterrevolutionary nucleus to form in the Vendée; finally, if you had arrested those who signed anticivic petitions, etc.,

etc. . . . And profiteers and speculators, aren't they every bit as guilty, if not more so? Like the others, aren't they veritable assassins of the nation?

So don't fear having the thunder of your justice burst over these vampires; don't fear making the people too happy. To be sure, they never calculated when it was a question of doing everything for you. They proved to you, notably on the days of May 31 and June 2, that they wanted total liberty. In exchange, give them bread and a decree; prevent the good people from being "put to the question ordinary and extraordinary" by the excessive price of comestibles.

Up to the present moment the big merchants, who are criminals through principles and accomplices of kings through habit, have abused the freedom of commerce to oppress the people; they have falsely interpreted that article of the *Declaration of the Rights of Man* that establishes that it is permitted to do all that is not forbidden by the law. Well then, decree constitutionally that speculation, the sale of minted money, and profiteering are harmful to society. The people, who know their true friends, the people who have suffered for such a long time, will see that you are saddened by their lot and that you seriously want to cure their ills. When they will have a clear and precise law in the constitutional act against speculation and profiteering they will see that the cause of the poor is closer to your hearts than that of the rich; they will see that there don't sit among you bankers, arms merchants, and profiteers; finally, they will see that you don't want the counterrevolution.

It is true that you have decreed a forced loan of one billion on the rich, but if you don't uproot the tree of speculation, if you don't put a national brake on the avidity of profiteers, then the very next day the capitalists and merchants will raise this sum from the sans-culottes through profiteering and fraud. It would thus not be the egoist, but the sans-culotte that you will have struck. Before your decree the grocery store owner and the banker ceaselessly pressured citizens. What vengeance will they not exact today, now that you make them pay? What new tribute will they not raise on the blood and tears of the unfortunate?

It will be objected in vain that the worker receives a salary in keeping with the increase in the price of goods. In truth there are some whose industry is better paid, but there are also many whose labor is less well paid since the Revolution. Besides, all citizens are not workers, and all workers are not occupied, and among those who are there are those with eight or ten children incapable of earning a living, and in general women don't earn more than twenty sous a day.

Deputies of the Mountain, if you would climb from the third to the ninth floor of the houses of this revolutionary city you would be touched by the tears and the sobs of an immense people, without bread or clothing, reduced to a state of distress and misfortune by speculation and profiteering, because laws have been cruel to the poor, because they were only made by and for the rich.

Oh rage, oh shame of the eighteenth century! Who could believe that the representatives of the French people, who declared war on the enemies without were so cowardly as to not crush those within? Under the reign of Sartine and Flesselles the government wouldn't have tolerated that goods of prime necessity be paid for at three time their value.[4] What am I saying? They even fixed the

---

4 Antoine de Sartine (1729–1801)—lieutenant general of the police under Louis XVI much hated by the people. Jacques de Flesselles (1721–1789)—provost of the merchants of Paris. Killed by the crowd the day the Bastille was seized.

price of arms and viands for the soldier. And the National Convention, invested with the force of twenty-five million men, will allow the merchant and the rich egoist to habitually bear it a mortal blow by arbitrarily taxing the things most useful to life? Louis Capet, in order to carry out the counterrevolution, had no need to provoke the wrath of foreign powers. The enemies of the Fatherland had no need to flood the departments of the west with a rain of fire: speculation and profiteering suffice to overturn the edifice of republican laws.

But, it will be said, it's the war that is the cause of the dearness of goods. Then why, representatives of the people, did you provoke it? Why, under the cruel Louis XVI, did the French have to repel the league of tyrants, and why didn't speculation spread over this empire the standard of revolt, of famine, and of devastation? And under this pretext the merchant is allowed to sell candles at six francs the pound, soap at six francs the pound, oil six francs the pound. Under pretext of war the sans-culotte will thus pay for shoes at fifty livres the pair, a shirt at fifty livres, a poor quality hat fifty livres. . . . So it can be said that the predictions of Cazalès and Maury have been fulfilled: in this case you will have conspired with them against the freedom of the Fatherland.[5] What am I saying? You will have surpassed them in treason. And so the Prussians and the Spaniards can say, "We are free to enchain the French, for they lack the courage to enchain the monsters that devour them"; and so we can say that in spreading around millions, in associating bankers and big merchants with

---

5 Jacques Antoine Marie de Cazalès (1758–1805) and Jean-Siffrein Maury (1746–1817) were both influential members of the Constituent Assembly and were defenders of royalist and traditionalist opinion. Both fled France in 1792.

the party of the counterrevolutionaries, the republic will destroy itself.

But it's paper, it can be said, that is the cause of the dearness of things. Ah, the sans-culotte doesn't see that there's much in circulation; in any event, its prodigious issuance is proof of its value and the price attached to it. If the assignat has a real value, if it rests on the loyalty of the French nation, the quantity of national effects sub-tracts nothing from their value. Just because there is much money in circulation, is that a reason to forget that we are men, to commit brigandage in taverns of commerce, to make oneself master of the fortunes and lives of citizens, to employ all means of oppression suggested by avarice and party spirit, to incite the people to revolt and force it, by famine and the torture of unfulfilled needs, to devour its own entrails?

But the assignats lose much in commerce. Why then do the internal and foreign bankers, businessmen, and counterrevolutionaries fill their coffers with them? Why do they have the cruelty to diminish the salaries of certain workers, and why don't they offer an indemnity to others? Why don't they offer a discount when they acquire national lands? Does England, whose debt exceeds the value of its territory twenty-fold, and which flourishes only on the paper of its bank, proportionally pay for its goods as dearly as we do? Ah, Minister Pith [*sic*] is too skillful to allow the subjects of George to be crushed in this way. And you, citizen representatives, you the depu-ties of the Mountain, you who boast of being among the numbers of the sans-culottes, from the height of your immortal rock you refuse to exterminate the constantly reborn hydra of speculation!

But, it is added, we get many articles from overseas, and they want only money in payment. This is false:

commerce is almost always carried out through exchange of merchandise for merchandise and paper for paper. In many cases goods are preferred over money. The metallic monies that circulate in Europe would not suffice to cover the one-hundred-thousandth part of the bills in circulation. So it is clear as day that speculators and bankers discredit assignats only in order to sell their money more dearly, to find the occasion to profiteer with impunity and to traffic at the counter in the blood of patriots they burn to spill.

But it isn't known how things will turn out. It's certain that the friends of equality will not always suffer that we have them slaughtered beyond the borders, and that within them they be besieged by famine. It's certain that they will not always be the dupes of that public plague, of the charlatans who eat away at us like worms: the hoarders whose storehouses are nothing but dens of swindlers.

But when the death penalty is pronounced against whoever will attempt to reestablish the royalty; when the countless legions of citizen soldiers form a vault of steel with their weapons; when they spit out saltpeter and fire from all sides on a horde of barbarians, can the baker and the hoarder say that they don't know how things will turn out? In any event, if they don't know it, we've come to tell them: *the people want freedom and equality, the republic or death*; and this is precisely what drives you to despair, vile henchmen of tyranny!

Not having succeeded in corrupting the heart of the people, in subjugating them through terror and calumny, you employ the last resources of slaves in order to stifle the love of liberty. You seize control of manufacturing and seaports, of all branches of commerce, of all the products of the land in order to make the friends of the Fatherland die of hunger, thirst, and lack of clothing, and to drive them to throw themselves into the arms of despotism.

But the knaves will not reduce to slavery a people that lives only by steel and liberty, privations, and sacrifices. It is reserved to partisans of the monarchy to prefer ancient chains and treasures to the republic and immortality.

And so representatives of the people, to demonstrate heedlessness much longer would be an act of cowardice, a crime of *lèse-nation*. You mustn't fear incurring the hatred of the rich, that is, the evil. You mustn't fear sacrificing political principles to the salvation of the people, which is the supreme law.

Agree with us then that it is through pusillanimity that you authorize the discrediting of paper; that you prepare bankruptcy by tolerating abuses and crimes before which despotism would have blushed in the last days of its barbarous power.

We know that no doubt there are evils that are inseparable from a great revolution; that there are sacrifices that must be borne to make liberty triumph; and that we cannot pay too dearly for the pleasure of being republicans. But we also know that the people have been betrayed by two legislatures; that the vices of the Constitution of 1791 were the source of public calamities, and that its time that the sans-culottes, who smashed the scepter of kings, see the end to insurrections and all types of tyranny.

If you don't quickly remedy this, how will those who have no estate, those who have only two, three, four, five, or six hundred livres in annuities—and this not well paid, either in land rents or personal accounts—how will they subsist if you don't stop the course of speculation and profiteering, and this by a constitutional decree that is not subject to the variations of legislatures? It's possible that we won't see peace for twenty years. The costs of the war will cause a new issuance of paper. Do you thus want to perpetuate our ills during this whole time by a tacit authorization of speculation and profiteering? This would be the means for expelling all foreign patriots and preventing the slave peoples from coming to France to breathe the pure air of liberty.

Is it not enough then that your predecessors, for the most part of infamous memory, left us the monarchy, speculation, and war without your leaving us unclothed, starving, and in despair? Must it be that the royalists and the moderates, under the pretext of the freedom of commerce, continue to devour manufactories and landed property, that they grab the fruits of the fields, the forests, and the vine, of the very skin of animals; and that under the protection of the law they still drink from cups gilded with the blood and tears of citizens?

Deputies of the Mountain: No! No! You will not leave your work in a state of imperfection. You will found the bases for public prosperity; you will not consecrate the general and repressive principles of speculation and profiteering; you will not give to your successors the terrible example of the barbarism of powerful men over the weak, of the rich over the poor. You will not end your career in infamy.

With this full confidence, receive here the new oath we swear to defend unto the grave: liberty, equality, and the unity and indivisibility of the republic and the oppressed sans-culottes of the departments.

Let them come, let them quickly come to Paris to solidify the ties of fraternity! Then we will show them those immortal pikes that overthrew the Bastille; those pikes that brought down in putrefaction the Commission of Twelve and the faction of statesmen; those pikes that will render justice to the intriguers and the traitors behind whatever mask they wear and of whatever country they inhabit. It's then that we will lead them to the young oak where the Marseillais and the sans-culottes of the departments abjured their errors and vowed to overturn the throne. Finally, it's then that we will accompany them to the sanctuary of the laws where, with a republican hand, we will show them the side that wanted to save the tyrant and the Mountain that pronounced his death.

Long live the truth, long live the National Convention, long live the French Republic!

(in the printed version of the speech, Roux continues)

After this exposé of the evidence I will ask of the National Convention, which I respect, of my cruelest enemies, whom I do not fear, of all the sans-culottes, whom I'll defend unto the grave; I'll ask them if I deserved the insults and the calumnies which journalists have poured over my head. There is nevertheless a reproach that they are right to make with impunity; that's that I am a priest. . . . Yes, unfortunately, my father gave me no other estate.

But if all priests had, like me, taken the civic oath without being forced; if like me, they had employed their time in striking down pride and fanaticism; if like me, they had exposed the crimes of the court at the moment when counterrevolution was going to break out; if like me, they had led Louis Capet to the scaffold; if all, like me, had made the commitment to soon wed a virtuous woman; if all, like me, had set out in pursuit of the traitors of the three legislatures; if all, like me, had signed the petition of the Champ de Mars and the one against the faction of statesmen; if all, like me, had declared that they did not hold with the pope who, at this time, is a counterrevolutionary and an assassin; if all, like me, had voted for the universal republic; finally, if all, like me, made religion consist in the happiness of our fellows; if they didn't know any other cult than that of the Fatherland, any other flame than that of liberty, then we would attack priests less relentlessly. In any event, Cazalès and Barnave weren't priests,[6] and they betrayed the cause of the people; Brissot and Barabaroux weren't priests and they wanted to save the tyrant; Manuel wasn't a priest and he received assignats from the court; and many others who play at being patriots aren't priests, and they starve the republic . . . but they won't put it in irons.

Journalists have too often covered me with insults for me not to patriotically resist oppression.

I will thus oppose a formidable arm against all those who call me a fanatic, bloodthirsty, a counterrevolutionary: the address I presented last May 31 at the National Convention under the banner of the Gravilliers Section, which had the honor of being inserted in the bulletin.

Note: When I attack profiteers and speculators I am far from including in this infamous class a great number of grocers and merchants who have rendered themselves praiseworthy by their *civisme* and their humanity.

---

6 Antoine Barnave (1761–1793)—leader of a faction sympathetic to the plight of Louis XVI and Marie Antoinette. Guillotined.

■ THE AGONY OF THE CRUEL ANTOINETTE

The agony of the cruel Antoinette.—The need to immediately guillotine the scoundrels imprisoned at the Luxembourg.—The mask torn from the rogues and intriguers in the Jacobin and Cordelier Clubs.

Such were the vile forces that the politicians played upon in the National Convention to absolve the tyrant; such is the perfidious and sly policy the ringleaders of that scoundrel faction use to save Brissot, Guadet, Vergniaud, Fauchet,[1] and the other apostles of federalism imprisoned at the Luxembourg from their execution.

Nevertheless, their crimes are written in characters of blood; it was through them that perfidious generals opened the gates of our frontiers; it was through them that five hundred thousand men were traitorously sacrificed; it was by them that civil war in the departments of the west and the south has been set alight; it was through them that the plans for treason, waste, and devastation were executed that have led the Fatherland to the edge of the abyss.

How, when all of France arises to demand vengeance for so many crimes, is it possible that the revolutionary tribunal has suspended for two months the sword of justice over these abominable beings, whose name history

---

1 All of these figures were Girondins, all of them guillotined.

will only pronounce while blushing? How is it possible that the cruel Antoinette, who surpassed in villainy the Medicis and Nero, that the cruel Antoinette, for whom the people swear an implacable hatred and whose existence is a public calamity, still breathes in a regenerated nation?

People, I am going to teach you why. It's that among those who are charged with pronouncing on the fate of the great guilty ones there are many who hold the strings of counterrevolution; it's that the judges are for the most part men of the robe, expert in the art of slipping conspirators away through the tortured folds of chicanery; it's that a large part of those who occupy public posts only serve the Revolution so as to pile up treasure on top of treasure. Everyone knows that the true guilty ones are the nobles and the *ci-devant* privileged. Nevertheless, all we see climb up to the scaffold are miserable domestics. The great knaves all escape the sword of the law. I defy you to cite me one profiteer who paid for his thefts, his larceny, and his fraud with his head. I defy you to cite me one deputy, one minister who has suffered the penalty the law inflicts on those who betray their Fatherland. Montanet was convicted of having altered the registers of the revolutionary tribunal he presided over. Was he punished for this prevarication? No. The reason is clear: it's that the wolves don't eat each other. The knaves hold each other by the hand and nothing resists the magical power of gold and assignats.

It's true that Custine took his head to the gallows,[2] but the threats of the National Convention were necessary, and

---

2   Adam Philippe de Custine (1742–1793)—revolutionary general, led the Army of the Rhine and the North, proclaimed that only a dictator—preferably a general—could save France. After suffering serious defeats he was arrested in connection with a campaign led by Hébert and Robespierre and guillotined.

it was necessary to place his judges between obligation and the guillotine in order to determine them to strike this scoundrel. Thus the money they'd received to absolve the traitor wasn't stolen, for they put off striking him down until the last minute, like certain surgeons who, when they have wounds to heal, make the illness continue until suppuration, in order to take his last sou from the poor patient.

After the efforts taken to save the ex-general, Custine, what faces won't our venerables make when it is a question of putting King Brissot, Chancellor Vergniaud, Plenipotentiary Guadet, Grand Chaplain Fauchet and the chiefs of the court of federalists on the hot seat? When it is a question of pronouncing on the fate of the queen of émigrés, the radiant and odoriferous Antoinette?

If all the judges resemble Roussillon, who found himself ill when the citizens of Orleans, the assassins of Bourdon, were condemned; if they are as little courageous as Obsan, who abandoned his post at the Commune during the insurrection of May 31; if they insist on following all the rules in order to convict only by written proofs the scoundrels with which the administration and the armies are full, they won't fail to whitewash the most daring criminals, but the law is precise . . . the people have arisen. . . . Public opinion, that inexorable judge, will render justice on the traitors. Yes, if the ministers of the law don't fulfill their obligations they'll learn that it is only one step from the capitol to the Tarpeian Rock. The blood of the tyrant cemented the nascent republic. It's necessary that head of his cruel spouse, of the infamous Antoinette, who was conceived in crime, who was raised in the school of crime, who has only lived by crime, finally falls under the blade of the law; it's necessary that the execution of the unfaithful representatives detained at Luxembourg frighten the slavers, the partisans of federalism, and the traitors who halted the course of liberty. It's necessary that the deputies of the three legislatures who sold the rights of the people, who starved it and killed it, be put to judgment without delay.

A great act of justice presents itself here, and that's to make the deputies who acquired a fortune in the last two years cough it up. When one has but a slight patrimony of fifteen livres to spend a day, it's impossible to have a splendidly garnished table, lackeys, a carriage, country houses, without having prostituted oneself to the aristocracy, or without having squandered the treasury of the republic.

Thus, those who show off an insolent luxury, who buy national domains and the furnishings of *ci-devant* royal houses, we can be sure without being slanderous that they've put their hands in the purse, that they conspired to deliver our forts, and that they are the secret friends of royalty.

And so I am execrated at the Jacobin and Cordelier clubs, which conceal so many intriguers, because I fix the people's gaze on the countless knaves who surround them, on the profiteers, the hypocrites, and the traitors with which the sections are filled, on the prideful representatives who only abolished royalty so as to take over the reins of government, to oppress the true patriots, and to gorge themselves on the blood of the people.

It's because I had the courage to tear the veil from intrigue and crime that they were barbaric enough, the scoundrels, to throw me into a dungeon that light didn't reach. Who could believe that Hébert, who said so many times at the Cordeliers Club and at the Commune that if all priests were like me they wouldn't be dangerous; that Hébert who many times celebrated my civic virtues, associated himself with my slanderers in order to destroy me in the spirit of the sans-culottes. Hébert, Chaumet, Robespierre,

Collot d'Herbois,[3] etc., etc., etc.: I render homage to your talents and your virtues, but I am forced to say that if you didn't fear the difficult truths that come from my pen you wouldn't so often exhale your bile against a priest who has rendered many services to the Revolution. Not one of my enemies thinks that I am an aristocrat; not one of them thinks me a moderate. What then is my crime? It's being exasperated, you say; it's taking *civisme* beyond all limits; it's compromising the republic by an exalted imagination.

Ah, if only most of the rogues who accuse me hadn't themselves changed principles; if there weren't some reproaches to be made of their management during the holding of the legislatures; if they hadn't conceived the perfidious design of oppressing liberty by taking over all powers, they wouldn't at every instant cast anathemas on an individual who wholeheartedly wants the happiness of the people, the unity and indivisibility of the republic. Men who mimic patriots, citizens who have rendered yourselves praiseworthy by your courage, occupy yourselves instead with saving the republic! It's not by piling denunciation on top of denunciation that you will expel the Austrians from our territory. Commodities are at an exorbitant price: work to bring it down! There are assassins, national thieves, profiteers: deliver them to the revolutionary tribunal; execute the terrible decree against speculation and hoarding; make the knaves who for the past three years surpassed in fraud the ministers and bloodsuckers of the ancient regime cough it up. Establish primary schools where citizens can come eat the bread of liberty; set in

---

3 Jean-Marie Collot d'Herbois (1749–1796)—member of the Committee of Public Safety, partisan of the Terror, and a leader in the crushing of rebellious Lyon. Despite this, one of the artisans behind the fall of Robespierre on 9 Thermidor.

motion workshops for the fabrication of arms of all sorts. Be the first to march against the enemy! These sublime movements of generosity, these courageous impulses will attest that you love the Fatherland for itself and not for the advantages it procures you. As for me, I declare that I have no other ambition but that of dying for the freedom of my country. I call on the rogues who ceaselessly slander me to put before me a vigorous test; they'll see that my blood clings to nothing, and that all my intrigue consists in unmasking traitors and braving daggers.

From *Le Publiciste de la République Francaise par l'ombre de Marat, l'Ami du Peuple*, no. 35 September 1, 1793.

■ INTERROGATION CONCERNING MARAT'S ASSASSINATION

Note by the historian Mortimer Ternaux: *When the news of Marat's assassination spread around Paris it occurred to no one that the assassin could be a woman, and the first suspected were those who had had differences with the Friend of the People. Among them was Jacques Roux, who was normally mixed up in intrigues as well as every street movement. Marat had bitterly attacked him in his journal at the time of the petition of the Gravilliers Section, and Jacques Roux hadn't hidden his irritation. For a period he was thought to have been capable of taking revenge, and we here give his interrogation before the Committee of General Safety. Jacques Roux had been denounced by the police observer Blache, whose letter follows:*

Police Report

Citizen Greive, who resides on rue Cimetière-Saint-André-des-Arts near Jardinet in the faubourg Saint-Germain at Citizen Denis's, last Tuesday was at Citizen Marat's along with Citizen Allain. While they were talking with the latter, Jacques Roux came into Marat's house. The latter spoke to him with all republican energy. Jacques Roux left, and from the doorway cast a look of fury mixed with indignation at Citizen Marat. This look surprised Greive and Allain. The latter also said a few things to Jacques Roux. Greive gave Citizen Allain's address.

Jacques Roux lives on rue Aumaire, at the Saint-Nicolas-des-Champs community of priests.

Prepared for the Committee of General Safety,
July 14, 1793, Year II of the Republic.
Blache.

The report was accompanied by a declaration signed by Citizens Allain and Greive of the Marseille Section, attesting to the profound impression they'd felt seeing Jacques Roux stop at the end of the long landing before going down the stairs, casting a prolonged vengeful look that was impossible to describe.

Jacques Roux was interrogated that very day, but Charlotte Corday had already been arrested and he was freed. In the interrogation we note how he disavows the petition that was the reason behind his expulsion from the Cordeliers Club.

Committee of General Safety
July 14, 1793, Year II of the Republic

Q: What is your name?
A: *Jacques Roux.*
Q: Where do you live?
A: *At Saint-Nicolas-des-Champs, Gravilliers Section.*
Q: What is your profession?
A: *I'm a priest and a municipal officer of Paris.*
Q: Did you know Marat?
A: *Yes, I knew him, and he found asylum at my house when he was persecuted by Lafayette.*
Q: Had it been a long time since you'd seen him when he was assassinated?

A: *I had been at his place five or six days ago, to bring him my baptismal certificate and a letter I'd written him asking him to retract what he'd said in some of his issues.*

Q: Was there anyone there when you entered his house?

A: *There were six people, more or less, to the best of my recollection.*

Q: Did you not have an argument with Marat?

A: *None.*

Q: What was the reason for your visit?

A: *It was to give him a letter, since I didn't count on finding him.*

Q: You didn't have a problem with him that day?

A: *No, none at all. He told me I was a hypocrite as far as I can recall.*

Q: When you left Marat's you didn't say anything unpleasant to him?

A: *No.*

Q: Did you ever write for or against the republic?

A: *I wrote only to defend and support it.*

Q: Did he say anything unpleasant to you?

A: *Yes, he advised me to go vegetate at my estate.*

Q: When you left Marat's did you not show, in you bearing and physiognomy, anything that revealed feelings against him?

A: *No.*

Q: What work did you propose to do against Marat?

A: *A response to one of his issues.*

Q: Did you know anything of an assassination plot against Marat?

A: *No.*

Executed and completed at the Committee of General Safety.

Citizen Jacques Roux, before signing, said that Marat attacked him in their conversation for having delivered a mortal blow to the republic in the address he'd presented at the bar of the Convention

*in the name of the Gravilliers Section around the end of last June.
To which he answered that such had not been his intention; that
the constitution being accepted he would conform to it and use all
of his means to defend and support it.*

Jacques Roux

From Mortimer Ternaux, *Histoire de la terreur* (Paris: M. Lévy Frères,
1868).

■ THE AWAKENING OF THE REVOLUTIONARY TRIBUNAL

The goodness of the French has increased the numbers of the enemies of the government and emboldened conspirators: it is this excess of indulgence that has served to have us slaughtered. By what fatality then has the Revolutionary Tribunal not yet questioned the cruel Antoinette, who covered France in blood and who is covered in crime. The concern shown for that Messaline shows that the judges believe in ghosts, that they are vile admirers of royalty and are perhaps even its accomplices. It seems that that scoundrel was transported from the tower of the Temple to the prisons of the palace only to remove her from the surveillance of the magistrates of the people, to provide her with the occasion to plot with traitors, to move the counterrevolutionaries by her lot, and to escape during a moment of troubles.

Nevertheless, there is no one who can doubt that that bloody harlot is not as much—if not even more—guilty than her barbarous husband. Have we forgotten that that atrocious woman had the sanctuary of nascent freedom invested with bayonets in '89; that she prepared the dissolution of the Estates General by force of arms; that she presided over the plotters who wanted to destroy Paris? Have we forgotten that the Austrian woman gave the order to her henchmen to fire on the people on the days of October 5 and 6; that at that time she said that she'd drink the blood of the French to the last drop with pleasure? Have we forgotten that that tigress had been connected with all that is impure and aristocratic among the slaves of the tyrant; that three times a week Leopold sent her couriers; and that it's through her channel that Montmorin, Guignard, La Luzerne, Duportail, Bertrand, Duport, Tessarts, Chambonas, Narbonne, Clavière, etc. were removed from the ministries? Have we forgotten the voyage to Montmédy,[1] and that to avenge her arrest she had the blood of patriots spilled on the Champ de Mars and armed eleven crowned brigands in order to revive the ancien régime? Have we forgotten that she was at the head of the counterfeiters of Passy, the profiteers of the Gironde and the isles of the Levant; that she only conferred the command of armies on knaves and assassins? Finally, have we forgotten that she constantly pulled the strings of counterrevolution, that she gave refuge in her apartments to the knights of the dagger, to refractory priests, to the most rotten aristocrats, and that on August 10, she had the Swiss Guards pass in review?

Ah! If, when the chateau of the Tuileries was taken, the victors had the right to kill Antoinette, the judges shouldn't hesitate to say to her: you are the sister of Leopold, who has massacred three hundred thousand French: you deserve death. . . . You are the widow of a tyrant, whose pen you guided: you deserve death. It's through you and your son that the counterrevolutionaries of Lyon, Marseilles, and the Vendée are armed: you deserve death. Go, cruel woman, expiate your crimes on the scaffold. Barbarous Antoinette, you will not have the pleasure of seeing half the nation slaughtered and the other half enchained.

---

1   City to which the royals intended to flee.

This is the language that the Revolutionary Tribunal should use with Custine for the conduct of this *ci-devant* noble in the Constituent Assembly; his relations with Lafayette, Dumouriez, and l'Egalité;[2] his correspondence with the King of Prussia; the abandonment of the army that was at his orders in the moment of crisis; the horrible despotism that he exercised toward patriotic officers and soldiers who he had executed for having frequented popular societies; the obstacles that he placed before the propagation of the principles of liberty; the immense artillery that he removed from Lille in order to put it at the disposal of the Prussians; the surrender of Condé, of Mainz, and of Valenciennes: these are proofs that suffice to lead him to the gallows. In those departments that are in a state of rebellion the friends of Liberty are led to the gallows without pity. They are sacrificed to the fury of despotism without the observation of any forms. Because Custine has committed all kinds of crimes; because his coffers are full of gold and assignats; because he has occupied eminent positions, must we fear striking him? In order to condemn this scoundrel it is enough to say to him that he was at the head of the best army of the republic and that he didn't come to the aid of our fortified places. It's enough to say to him that the department of the Nord is practically invaded, that Cambrai is perhaps encircled, and the enemy advances with great speed toward Paris; it's enough to say to him that being by nature and habit the enemy of the people, he wasn't able to defend their cause, and consequently he betrayed. His head should thus fall under the sword of the law.

---

2   Louis Philippe II, Duke of Orleans (1747–1793)—member of the royal family who joined the revolutionary cause. Guillotined after Dumouriez's flight on suspicion of having been in league with him.

There is a no less rigorous measure to be taken toward the conspirators: it's to take their wives and children as hostages until the triumph of liberty; it's to expel from public employment the nobles and all those who clung to the privileged castes. This desire of the French is pronounced with such energy that the National Convention will doubtless not delay in bringing to justice the nobles, who are spies, thieves, and assassins.

I even think that we will soon be forced to arrest them. Here is a recent event that will serve to enlighten public opinion.

The Committee of Public Safety of the city of Angoulême (department of the Charente) had incarcerated some suspects in their district. Lords Garat and Chabrefy, well known for their *incivisme*, were arrested, as were sixty-seven other individuals like them. Such is the aristocracy of the department and the municipality that Procureur Souchet and Mayor Reynier immediately freed the counterrevolutionaries.

I denounce another despotic measure that the administrator Jobert has just executed in Paris. Citizen Jean-Charles Cosfin—employee at the office of public contributions at the *mairie* on rue Philippeau, no. 220—guided by sentiments of humanity, presented himself two days ago to the police to testify to the interest he'd taken in the situation of a woman who, nursing her baby and her eyes full of tears, had begged him to facilitate the task of informing her husband of some domestic affairs.

This administrator rejected with disdain the representations of Citizen Cosfin in favor of that unfortunate woman whose husband had been incarcerated a few days before. Jobert imperiously ordered the guards to show him the door. Barely had the citizen responded that that he was going to leave, but that he wouldn't fail to give an account of this outrageous conduct, than the virtuous Jobert had the shamelessness to have him arrested in the prison of the *mairie* in contempt of all claims, without even accepting to hear the administrator of public contributions, which Citizen Cosfin had requested.

The law will doubtless bring to justice such an abuse of authority. When even one of its members is oppressed there is oppression against the whole social body. Liberty will soon be wiped out if an individual arrogates to himself the right to incarcerate another, if a committee unites within it several powers, if it sets itself up as a central committee in government, if we put at its disposal a sum of fifty million. History teaches us that the Roman senators didn't delay in enchaining the people once they had themselves granted a civil list. . . . It is the gold of the defunct tyrant that has attracted so many ills to our unfortunate Fatherland.

From *Le Publiciste de la République Française par l'ombre de Marat*, no. 256, August 14, 1793.

ANACHARSIS CLOOTS (1755–1794)

■ RELIGION IS THE GREATEST OBSTACLE

Will you allow me, citizen colleagues, to put you in a position to repair an outrage to reason committed by the Legislative Assembly, which, on the Christian observations of the Bishop of Calvados of guillotined memory, put off the reception of one of my philosophical productions, the fruit of fifteen hours of work daily for four straight years? This work, unique in its methods and tactics and interesting in its details and development, with one blow undermined all revealed religions, both ancient and modern. It is entitled *The Certainty of the Proofs of Mohammedanism*, for I throw a Muslim at the legs of other sectarians, who fall one after the other. My book takes the place of a vast library.

The philosophical explosion that strikes our revolutionary gaze is the result of fifty years of labor and persecution. It is by attacking all false revelations with courageous tenacity that we have arrived at the revelation of good sense. The conversion of a great people proves that philosophers have not planted in barren soil and that the proselytism of error is less rapid than that of eternal principles. It is today that the benedictions of truth make us forget the maledictions of falsehood. I am glad to have been persecuted by an Archbishop of Paris when I see the entire clergy of France abjure a doctrine against which I threw volumes ten years before the taking of the Bastille.

Under the reign of kings and priests I was never forgiven my favorite motto: *Veritas atque Libertas.*

I owe to my continual voyages and my independent cosmopolitanism the fact that I have escaped the vengeance of sacred and profane tyrants. I was in Rome when they wanted to incarcerate me in Paris, and I was in London when they wanted to burn me in Lisbon. It was by shuttling from one end of Europe to the other that I was able to escape the hired assassins and informants of all masters and valets. The Revolution has finally arrived, and I am in my natural element, for *it is liberty and not the place that makes the citizen,* as Brutus so aptly said, and as our rapporteur on the law against foreigners has so clearly forgotten.[1] I too was ungrateful enough to forget the cradle of my birth in thinking only of the cradle of the Universal Republic—if spreading enlightenment in the capitol of the world means forgetting your native land. Whatever the case, my emigration came to an end when the emigration of the villains began. Regenerated Paris was the post of the "Orator of the Human Race," and I haven't quit it since 1790.

It was then that I redoubled my zeal against the so-called sovereigns of heaven and earth. I loudly preached that there is no other God but nature, no other sovereign than the human race: the people-God. This people is self-sufficient in meeting its own needs. It will forever stand: nature doesn't kneel. Judge the majesty of the free human race by that of the French people, which is but a fraction of it. Judge the infallibility of all by the sagacity of a portion, which on its own is making the slave world tremble. The more the mass of free men grows, the less will great personages be

---

1   Saint-Just, who had presented and had adopted a law ordering that foreigners born subjects of governments the republic was at war with would be detained until peace was declared.

feared. The suspect will disappear with tyrants. Universal leveling stands in opposition to all forms of rebellion. The Surveillance Committee of the Universal Republic will have less work than the committee of the least Paris section. Such shall be the case for all ministerial offices. My republic is the antidote for bureaucracy: there will be few offices, few taxes, and no executioners. General confidence will replace a necessary mistrust. Reason will unite all men in one representative fasces, with no other connection than epistolary correspondence. This will be the true republic of letters.

Citizens, religion is the greatest obstacle to my utopia. But beyond a doubt, this obstacle is not invincible, for we see Christians and Jews dispute the honor of the most solemn abjuration. It will be the same everywhere that the Mountain's constitution is accepted, everywhere that men have five senses. A constitution that leaves nothing to priests but their mummeries, forcing them to restore our morality and money to us, by showing imposture in its horrifying nudity, will accomplish without cease the marvels that now pass before our eyes. And this is even more the case because the requisition of men and things is leading all spirits toward the theater of the war of liberation.

I will not refute the illogic of those who see counterrevolutionary intrigues in this and who imagine that we are leading the people to a precipice. Rest assured, good people, that the people do not allow themselves to be led; they have burned their ties and know more than all the doctors in the world. As for the disguised aristocrats who repeat their old slanders against the central Commune, adding that the departments aren't mature, I send them to the Nièvre, the Somme, to Rochefort, to Ris, etc.,[2] unless

---

2 Regions where the dechristianization movement was especially strong.

they would prefer a stay in the Vendée, whose holy furies have accelerated the healing of our victorious republicans. Note, citizens, that most of those who now play the role of tremblers were the first to condemn the prudence of the Jacobins, who last fall opposed the premature motion of a member of the Finance Committee.[3] And these same Jacobins, always ready to catch the ball on the rebound, rise today to crush the religious hydra-head for good and all. A salutary terror is dissipating all fantastic terrors. An ancient said: "We only possess vigor the first day following a bad reign." Let us profit from this first day, which we will prolong until the day after the deliverance of the world.

It is thus recognized that the adversaries of religion have deserved well of the human race. It is in keeping with this that I request a statue in the Temple of Reason for the first ecclesiastical abjurer. It will suffice to give his name to obtain a favorable decree from the National Convention: it is the intrepid, the generous, the exemplary Jean Meslier, curate of Etrépigny in the Champagne, whose *Testament* brought desolation to the Sorbonne and among all Christ-lovers. The memory of this honest man, condemned under the ancien régime, should be rehabilitated under nature's regime.

Citizen colleagues, you will honorably receive my two proposals, for the archbishops of Paris and the bishops of the Calvados are no longer on the order of the day.

Speech pronounced at the Tribune of the National Convention, 27 Brumaire, Year II [November 17, 1793].

---

3 Cambon, who had proposed in November 1792 removing the expenses of the Catholic religion from the 1793 budget.

■ SPEECH GIVEN IN THE NAME OF THE PRUSSIAN *FÉDÉRÉS*

August 12, 1792

Legislators:

There would be no slaves left on earth if the text of your law was understood by the troops of men groaning beneath the rod of a few men called kings. Monarch's thrones are miserable trestle tables in the eyes of the man who has read the seventeen articles of the *Declaration of Rights*. Never has a crown-wearer, a crowned executive power, been anything but a disorganizing power.

The delirium of tyrants obliges you to spread enlightenment, weapons in hand. You have wisely conceived the project of forming different foreign legions. These phalanxes of interpreters, these bellicose dragomen, will deal death to oppressors and give life to the oppressed. Translators of universal law, they will dissipate the shadows that hide the impostures of royalty from the sight of nations. The petitioners who have your attention at this moment have sworn the deliverance of their Penates. Prussians, they promise to attract to their side the satellites of a Brandenburgian Sardanopolis. Legislators, we offer you a Prussian legion.

This brave Vandal, who you see covered with honorable scars, is a colonel whose merit Frederick the Great was

able to distinguish in long and famous wars. The uncon-
cern and ingratitude of Friedrich Wilhelm, the hereditary
hatred toward us of the House of Austria, the love that
we hereditarily have for the French, the natural horror of
despotism, all inspire the most just of vengeances in this
warrior whose name is dear to the conquerors of Silesia.

All enlightened Prussians share the sentiments of
Prince Heinrich, of Generals Möllendorf, Kalckreuth, and
Sheffen. The opinion of Minister Hertzberg, who was at
first undecided, is decidedly favorable to France. Berlin
and Paris are perfectly in agreement in their aversion
to the tyrants of Lorraine. As the treasury of the Spree
is exhausted public opinion will grow stronger, and the
heroism of the French people will triumph over the idiocy
of the court at Potsdam.

The philosophy of Voltaire and Rousseau put down
too solid roots under a glorious forty-six-year reign for the
Fatherland of Copernicus, the capitol and refuge of the
reformers of Germany and France, to ally itself with Austria
in order to reestablish papistry and Machiavellianism on
the banks of the Seine. A dull murmur is making itself heard
in all Protestant countries. The Duke of Brunswick himself
is overwhelmed with dark thoughts on the fate of his religion and his principality. Will the King of Prussia, more
gallant than his predecessor, persist in ruining himself for
two women, for Antoinette of Lorraine and Catherine of
Russia? Prussian officers are too reasonable and too educated to ignore the true interests of Brandenburg. They
deplore the ineptitude of a crazed king by invoking the
manes of a philosopher king and by turning their gaze
toward the heir presumptive, who openly protests against
the absurd league of Pillnitz. The Prussian soldier will half-
heartedly fight for imperials he hates and for émigrés he
holds in contempt. There is not a single family in Prussia

who doesn't have some reason to seek vengeance for the barbarian policies of Vienna, Versailles, and Petersburg.

Two great errors give birth to most of our ills: the fraudulent sovereignty of princes and the partial sovereignty of peoples. The moment has arrived to repatriate all members of the human family through the promulgation of the eternal principle of the indivisible sovereignty of the human race. The rights of man are the same everywhere: one law, one sovereign. Without this salutary principle the least hamlet could make itself into a sovereign, sadly isolate itself, and spread discord on the earth. But with this luminous and fecund principle, with this first commandment of nature, an unalterable harmony will cover the globe with all the benefits of perpetual peace.

Legislators, our Prussian *fédérés* ask you for a military regime. We know all the byways and exits of the Hercynian Forest: we will be more fortunate than Varus. You will never have to ask a second time for a legion invincible through the ascendancy that truth has over lies, and freedom over slavery. Say the word and we will be off.

■ SPEECH ON BEHALF OF THE COMMITTEE OF FOREIGNERS

The imposing fasces of all the flags of the French Empire that are to be deployed on July 14 on the Champ de Mars, in the same place that Julian crushed all prejudices, where Charlemagne surrounded himself with all virtues, this civic solemnity will be not only the festival of the French but, even more, the festival of the human race. The trumpet that sounded the resurrection of a great people has reverberated in the four corners of the globe, and the songs of joy of twenty-five million free men have awakened peoples buried under a long period of slavery. The wisdom of your decrees, messieurs, the unity of the children of France, this ravishing tableau causes despots bitter worries, and just hopes in enslaved nations.

To us too has come a great thought, and we dare say it will complement the great national day! A number of foreigners from all the countries of the earth ask to be allowed to line up in the middle of the Champ de Mars, and the Liberty Bonnet they'll joyfully raise will be the guarantee of the imminent deliverance of their unhappy fellow citizens. At Roman triumphs they were all too happy to drag the vanquished behind their chariots. You, honorable messieurs, in the most honorable of contrasts, you will see in your cortege free men whose Fatherlands are in chains, and whose Fatherlands will be free one day under the influence of your unshakeable courage and philosophical laws. Our vows and our homage will be the bonds attaching us to your triumphal chariots.

Never was there a more sacred ambassadorship. Our letters of appointment aren't written on parchment; our mission is engraved in ineffaceable characters in the hearts of all men. And thanks to the authors of the *Declaration of Rights* these characters will no longer be unintelligible to tyrants.

Messieurs, you have genuinely recognized that sovereignty resides in the people. Everywhere the people are under the yoke of dictators who, despite your principles, call themselves sovereigns. Dictatorship is usurped, but sovereignty is inviolable, and the ambassadors of tyrants cannot honor your august festival as can most of us whose mission was tacitly acknowledged by our compatriots, by the oppressed sovereigns.

What a lesson for despots! What consolation for unfortunate peoples when we will teach them that the first nation of Europe, in gathering together its banners, gave us a sign of the happiness of France and the two worlds!

We will await, messieurs, in a respectful silence, the result of your deliberations on our petition, dictated to us by the enthusiasm of universal liberty.

Response of the president to the deputations of the different foreign countries:

Messieurs:
You have today proved to the entire universe that the progress made in philosophy and in the knowledge of the rights of man by one nation equally belongs to other nations. It has been shown that there are eras that influence the happiness and the unhappiness of all parts of the globe, and France dares today to flatter itself that

the example it has just given will be followed by those peoples who, knowing how to appreciate liberty, will teach monarchs that their true grandeur consists in commanding free men and executing laws, and that they can only be happy by causing the happiness of those who chose them to govern.

Yes, messieurs, France will honor itself in admitting you to the civic festival whose preparation the National Assembly has just ordered. But as the price for this beneficence, it believes it has the right to demand of you strong testimony of your recognition.

After the august ceremony, return to the places of your birth. Tell your monarchs, tell your administrators, whatever name they bear, that if they are jealous of passing their memory on to the most distant posterity, tell them that they have only to follow the example of Louis XVI, the Restorer of French Liberty.

The National Assembly invites you to participate in its session.

JACQUES HÉBERT (1757–1794)

■ IMPORTANT ADVICE FROM PÈRE DUCHESNE TO THE ARISTOCRATS

June 1790

I am gentle . . . a thousand million bombs. . . . I'm a fucking honest patriot. It's true, it's like that. But fuck! To play dead, to keep my mouth shut when a heap of troublemaking buggers like you look to turn France into a field of carnage and horror; when by the most execrable maneuvers to try to fool, to seduce, this so good, so wise people when it is doing nothing but following its heart's impulses; when you buy off fucking foreign scoundrels in order to make horrific fanaticism pullulate in our provinces; when you arm their ferocious and bloodthirsty hands with daggers; when you make a thousand attempts to dissolve our august learned assembly; when you want to put back on our bodies the shameful irons that our energy smashed. Oh triple name of a cannonade! It's not Père Duchesne who'll remain quiet when he learns of such horrors. I would be a madman, a cowardly gentleman, a bad priest, a wicked judge, or an infamous beggar if I acted like that. But no, thank god, me, I'm patriotic. I am, I've proved it, I'll talk about it, and I'll set my heart free. Too bad for the guilty, I could give a good goddamn.

Isn't it shameful, name of the depths of the hold, to see a gang of Tartuffes with black and perfidious souls circulate seditious letters, incendiary pastoral advisories, insulting protests, atrocious libels throughout the kingdom. Why? Yes, why? Five hundred million rammed bullets, why? Because, fat and greasy like pigs from the Auvergne, the dreadful power to make people die from indigestion has been taken from them. Because the nation is justly taking back an immense good that their deceitful founders had sacredly swindled from the imbecilic superstition of our fathers. And even more, we've left most of them a well-off existence and to most of them, *morbleu*, enough to feed twenty families of honest and useful artisans. And even so, they complain, they caw. Oh, double starboard! A scrap of tissue, a sack, a crust of bread, and some good clear water of the Seine from the point of the Île Saint-Louis, that's all you need. Fuck! Is that much given to the poor, and did Christ's disciples have more? And what's the difference between the former and the latter? The latter founded an admirable and sublime religion and the former dishonor it. The latter, who numbered twelve, with hair shirts and ashes on their heads, their waists cinched by crude leather belts, traveled the universe, which they educated with their learned and holy maxims, while the former claim that in reducing the French monarchy to ninety-three bishoprics the new bishops could no longer validly absolve sins and that in order to fulfill their holy ministry they need wigs, bright garb, sumptuous equipages, grand lackeys, magnificent hotels, beautiful mistresses, white and red wine, and may the devil take them far, far away, so we never hear from them again.

I'm getting carried away, but am I wrong? Is it possible to look on this with tranquility? I don't want to swear, four thousand million mortar guns, but is this good? Is this just? Do they need all this vainglory, all these pompoms, all these luxurious pleasures? Do the ministers of a god born in a stable need to have palaces?

And these proud nobles, these voracious bloodsuckers, their worthy friends through thick and thin, how can they be portrayed? Oh name of a cannonade, if only I had the pen of the *moderateur*, of the editor of the *Actes des apôtres*, or the gazetteer of Paris, patriotic writers, excellent, sublime, and who, probably, I hope, will one day receive the just reward of their civic labors. How I'll reveal their odious intrigues, their antipatriotic cabals, the perfidious goal they propose by spreading gold around and particularly to base journalists who back them up, and even more particularly who the famous authors I just named know, I'm sure of it. Good god, how I'll portray them. But while waiting for someone else to do the work, I'll ask these insolent nobles: What is the reason for your despair? Is it because the rights you usurped and that were our shame were abolished? Is it because the virtuous and enlightened artisan now has a claim to the positions, the dignities that you unjustly and exclusively arrogated to yourselves and that you so poorly filled and that you dishonor? Is it because your absurd privileges were destroyed, because you are forced to pay the nation the tax that every individual owes it and that you had found the perfidious and handy secret to exempt yourself from? In the past if your ancestors didn't pay them they raised at their own expense a company of soldiers and flew to the assistance of their oppressed country. But you have long forgotten their noble example. The warriors are in our pay, and they alone rescue the Fatherland; their blood alone reddened the battlefield and you were only at their head for vain display or to reap the glory of their noble acts, leaving them the suffering and the danger.

And those serious judges with their weighty, pompous air who, like aerostatic balloons, once wanted to float in the ethereal regions, finding the limits the heavens prescribed too narrow, see what angles they employ, what routes they take to reach their aristocratic colleagues and, at the same time, obtain the protection of the people who have, against their interests, so effectively served them in so many circumstances but who, now recognizing their odious egoism, cry out along with me: your suppression is just. Every time your interests were tied to ours you defended our cause and made it triumph. But you abandoned and even sacrificed it when our interests were no longer yours. Without the territorial tax you would have registered that of the stamp. Fortunately, you didn't do it: your greed, your vile egoism, better served us than your friendship. We are free and we would still be slaves.

Clergy, nobility, magistracy who, thank heaven, our courage, and the National Assembly, are no longer anything, but who, through your number, your pernicious maxims, your gold illicitly acquired, and your gangrened hatred for justice are still a danger to reason and order and are hatching the aristocratic seed of an impossible counterrevolution; ex-triumvirate, tyrannical, and fateful oppressor, listen to the sage advice of Père Duchesne, put it in practice or, a thousand million cannons loaded to the brim, be afraid of being laid flat in the register of the famous Desmoulins, attorney general of the lantern.

To the decrees of the National Assembly
Submit blindly

> The work of the constitution
> Trouble hardly
> Of your haughty airs
> Rid yourself entirely
> What you stole
> Return promptly
> For your vile deeds

Act repentantly
Become if you can
Friendly and like a family
Love and serve god
Saintedly
Spare us the horror
Of seeing you frequently
To a corner of the kingdom
Go quickly
End your days there
Infernally
When we hear you're dead
We'll do so happily
And I will cease to speak
Vulgarly

Père Duchesne, furnace-maker, heating engineer, and active citizen

■ THE GRAND ARMY OF PÈRE DUCHESNE TO GO FIGHT THE PRINCE DE LAMBESC, WHO IS AT THE HEAD OF SEVENTY THOUSAND AUSTRIANS WHO WANT TO ENTER FRANCE

ca. 1791

We shouldn't wait, my friends, for the Revolution to be made. Double millions of bombs and sabers, we shouldn't wait for the counterrevolutionaries to free us of our obligations. The damn bastards are plotting and cooking up new conspiracies. Like spiders who weave their webs every night, they dream only of the best way to slaughter us, to quench their thirst on our blood. Do you know what they're up to at this moment? Name of an anvil that falls on your head from a hundred feet, I'm going to educate you about their infernal scheme and of the damn lunch they are preparing for us, and then I'll tell you about the great project I cooked up so that they'll end up swallowing it themselves.

A thousand million thunders! The aristocrats are sly as foxes and wicked as wolves. These jackasses know that in order to make a counterrevolution you have to do two things: attack the patriots with an army from within and an army from without. Well then, the damn rascals have succeeded in having both of them. Within France and especially in the capital they buy off and enlist all the swindlers, all the bandits, and all the unfortunates who are forced by poverty to sell themselves. They are masters of a large part of the professional guard: even some of the brave victors of the Bastille are in their pay because of need and carry out the base profession of squealers. Double name of a lighted furnace! All these damn watchdogs are paid to descend on us at the first occasion and we're surrounded by assassins.

On the other hand, my comrades, learn, thunder of god, that the execrable swordsman of the Tuileries, the great sinner de Lambesc,[1] was named general of the Austrian troops and that he's on the banks of the Rhine at the head of seventy thousand men who are going to throw themselves on France and the Brabant. Learn, double millions of dives full of drunks, that the damn rascal de Mirabeau-Tonneau[2] shines in this army and blows into it as much poison as a thousand whores blow in a year into the bellies of the johns that pay them a visit. Learn that the men it is composed of are Hussars born in Croatia who are as ferocious as tigers and who, in the Turkish wars, put districts for

---

1 Charles Eugène, Prince of Lambesc (1751–1825)—peer of France and prince of Lorraine, after defending the Tuileries Palace against the people he fled France to lead the Bourbon armies against the Revolution.

2 André Boniface Louis Riqueti, Vicomte de Mirabeau (1754–1792)—brother of the orator, Honoré Mirabeau, he served in America during the War of Independence and violently opposed the Revolution, joining the émigré army based in Germany. He was commonly called Mirabeau-Tonneau (Mirabeau-Barrel) because of his taste for drink.

twenty leagues around to the torch, singing and smoking on the still palpitating corpses. Learn, finally, triple millions of volcanoes who swallow them up, that every day the native scoundrels of France, who sell themselves, go to join these seventy thousand men.

These then, my friends, are the two great traps that the infernal aristocracy is laying for you. Seventy thousand swordsman are heading toward Luxembourg with the braggart de Lambesc at their head, and the sack of wine de Mirabeau and a hundred thousand assassins and executioners are scattered among you under the mask of patriotism. Oh holy name of a thousand crushed skulls, what is to be done to protect ourselves from the storm that threatens us? As for me, thunder of a thousand gods, this is what I'm going to do.

The first time I hear that the jackass de Lambesc's army has entered the sacred soil of our country I'm going to go to Saint-Denis and take up Charlemagne's fearsome sword and put on his helmet and armor. Equipped with these shining emblems of victory, double millions of whores in rut, I'll climb on a table at the Palais-Royal, scimitar in hand, and I'll invite, with the voice of a thousand thunders augmented with the noise of a hundred thousand cannons, all the patriots, all the enemies of the ancien régime, to join me to rescue the Fatherland in danger and to fucking fight against the aristocrats and bastards of the Austrian clique.

Fuck! At the head of all these good people who never drank the water of the Machine de Marly or breathed the bad air of the prisons,[3] first I take hold of all the cannons and all the magazines that are in the capital. I decimate

---

3   The Machine de Marly was invented to provide the water for the fountains at the palace of Versailles. It used as much water as the city of Paris daily.

the National Guard of all the aristocrats, swindlers, and squealers it's infected with, and I'll send them to empty the privies at the Château of the Tuileries or dig a big hole there to throw in there the robes of all the magistrates, the skullcaps of the entire clergy, the safes of all the financiers, and all the parchments and quills of the defunct nobility.

After these essential preliminaries, double millions of cutoff ears and crushed noses, I'll march with my five hundred thousand good patriots against the jackass, the son of a bitch de Lambesc, may the devil swallow his body and Saint Michel digest his soul. Along the way I'll lock up for a hundred years the executioner de Bouillé,[4] who turned Nancy into a cemetery, and I'll avenge that unhappy city by giving the inhabitants all the booty, by suspending from its doors the skin of all the hussar hangmen and other enemies of France whose bellies my soldiers would have cut open or whose brains they would have smashed.

When I arrive on the banks of the Rhine and see the buggers who march under the banner of a mad dog like de Lambesc and a barfly like Mirabeau I'll line up my army for battle with the same skill that I set up my furnace pipes, and I'll harangue them thusly: Comrades, there are the watchdog-slaves who want to take our freedom from us. Show them people are a thousand times stronger and braver when they're free. Grind half of them to dust so that the others take on our sentiments and learn they must be dumber than animals, than horses, to fight for the pleasure of their tyrants.

With my courage and that of my companions, triple millions of devils drowned or roasted, I'll crush like a

---

4   François Claude Amour, marquis de Bouillé (1739–1800)—French royalist general, involved in the failed 1791 flight of the royal family. Died in exile in London.

grain of mustard the Austrian army that is advancing on Luxembourg, and I'll capture the bastard de Mirabeau and the bandit de Lambesc.

I'll sentence one to remain for eighty years on the horse of fame that's on the drawbridge of the Tuileries, where he cut down three men. As for the other one, his punishment will be to spend fifty years with his mouth open under the water-filled basin of the Samaritaine.

And so, my friends, fear nothing. You have brave men among you. Keep an eye on the ruses of the fake patriots and victory is ours.

■ THE GREAT ANGER OF PÈRE DUCHESNE AGAINST THE MODERATES

1793

Against the moderates who use whatever is at hand to oppose the execution of the revolutionary decree and to save the aristocrats and the conspirators. His good advice to all honest republicans so that they all put their heads in a bonnet in order to execute the law of the maximum and that which confiscates the property of suspects.

Oh fuck! How hard it is to kill the aristocracy. When it's about to receive the coup de grâce it plays dead, and when it looks to be crushed it revolts and comes back to life to posit out its poison with even greater force. Every day it gives birth to new monsters to torment the people. Goddammit, why do the patriots always stop halfway? Why, when they're in the process of striking, do they not exterminate all their enemies at once? Everything would have been over on August 10 if some indolent buggers hadn't stopped the avenging arm of the people. The ogre Capet and his abominable race would have lost the taste for bread, not a single chevalier of the dagger would have escaped. With one sweep of the net all the Feuillants,[1] all

---

1   The Club des Feuillants, officially the Friends of the Constitution, a group of constitutional monarchists.

the royalists, all the aristocrats would have been removed from Paris, and the departments that would have desired this great day as much as we would have copied us. But on the contrary the sans-culottes let themselves be fooled by two-faced jackasses. Moderatism carried the day. And, goddammit, what happened? The Brissotins ruled the roost. Old Roland, with the millions the Convention confided to him to purchase subsistence goods, schemed at counterrevolution. The boudoir of the whore who put horns on him replaced the Austrian committee. His squealers, dispersed all around the republic, lit the flame of civil war. Almost all the journalists sold out to that infamous clique and poisoned public opinion. The best citizens were dragged in the mud. Pure and courageous legislators passed for scoundrels. Those who had destroyed tyranny were accused of wanting to reestablish it. The voice of truth was stifled by lies and slander. There was no longer any safety for the small numbers of writers who had remained faithful to the people. Marat was looked upon as a werewolf. He passed for a ferocious beast and in several departments it was asked how many little children he ate for lunch and how many pints of blood he drank per day. Nevertheless, goddammit, there was no one in the republic as humane as he. The jackasses who wanted to be shed of him at whatever cost brought him up on charges, and in order to more surely assassinate him they cooked up the plot to kick off the revolutionary tribunal in order to create another made up of rascals and brigands like themselves. But, fuck, the sans-culottes fought back. The people defended the cause of their real friend and they didn't allow the Brissotins the time to commit their crime. Marat appeared before his judges and he confounded his accusers. Returned in triumph to the heights of the holy Mountain, he horrified all the wretches.

Fuck! While a handful of brave Montagnards confronted the storm and braved all dangers to save the republic, the infamous Dumouriez, in agreement with the Brissotins, led his soldiers to the slaughter and sold Belgium to the Austrians. At the same time Roland and his wife preached federalism, armed the departments against Paris and were already cooking up the war of the Vendée, goddammit! In order to deliver the coup de grâce to freedom, the damn gambling den called the Committee of Twelve was dreamed up. It was in the mire of the swamp that he went to get the toads and snakes it was made up of. The death of all the patriots was decided on. You remember, poor furnace merchant, that the dance was going to begin with you. For, at all times, goddammit, you were always the first one they had in their sights. Before that the Austrian committee had also wanted your skin, and the Feuillants had sworn that your head would be the first gift they'd offer the Austrian she-wolf. When the sack is too full it has to burst, goddammit! The events of May 31 were the second act of the tragedy of August 10. It saved the republic, and it led the main leaders of the conspiracy to the gallows. But fuck, all is not destroyed. Since they dared demand the opening of the prisons, the aristocrats have used everything in their power to free their friends and relatives and to destroy the patriots. Carra and Gorsas are resuscitated; the same infamies they produced are repeated by other prigs like them. The biggest conspirators find men bold enough to praise and defend them, and the best patriots, slandered, persecuted, dragged into dungeons, and mixed with the rogues, aristocrats, and royalists are cowardly abandoned or, if men just enough, daring enough, are found to defend them they are accused of being the leaders of the party, ambitious, disorganizers. Pitt's gold circulates freely in order to incite disorders, to sustain corruption, to protect crime, and to overwhelm innocence and virtue.

It's not only the patriots they want to destroy, god-dammit! It's the republic. The Feuillants, the newly made Brissotins, at the same time that they spread the poison of moderatism dare to condemn the revolutionary meas-ures that saved liberty. They secretly sap the government in order to take it over. A Committee of Public Safety, a Committee of General Safety composed of Philippotins would be the aristocracy's masterpiece.[2] Soon new toads would splash around in the marsh, soon a deadly combat would start up again between crime and virtue. And yet this is what certain rascals haven't feared to demand.

And it's on the eve of the great cleanup, at the moment when our brave warriors are burning with impatience to exterminate the slaves of despots, that put spokes in the wheels. Yes, goddammit, the patriots are right to express their indignation at seeing such plots being formed. The republic must be saved, and in order to save it justice must be rendered on all the scoundrels, intriguers, and conspirators.

Brave sans-culottes, you shouldn't throw out the baby with the bath water. Those who preach moderation are your worst enemies. Fuck! No more retreating! The Revolution must be completed. The Convention just rendered a new decree on the maximum that will kill the hoarders and bring back abundance. The law that confiscates the prop-erty of suspects and orders their deportation will take from the enemies of the people the means of troubling the peace and purge the republic of all the monsters who poison it. And so, dammit, in order to triumph over all cabals and all intrigues all true republicans must continue to surround

---

2   Philippotins: Followers for the former prince Philippe d'Orleans, who renamed himself Philippe Egalité and supported the Revolution.

the Convention, which is working tirelessly for the happiness of the people. Let all the sans-culottes rally to deliver it from all the traitors who conspire against liberty. Their number is yet great but, fuck, if the revolutionary laws are promptly and vigorously executed they will vanish into the void. I can't repeat this often enough: the cause of all the troubles that agitate us comes from the indulgence we've shown in the punishing of traitors. One step back would destroy the republic. So goddammit let us swear the death of the moderates, like that of royalists and aristocrats. With unity, courage, and steadfastness and all our enemies will be at *quia*, goddammit!

■ THE GREAT ANGER OF PÈRE DUCHESNE AGAINST THE RICH

1793

Against the rich who want to starve the people by hoarding wheat and supplies. His good advice to the Convention so that it raises an army of ten thousand sans-culottes in every department to force the big farmers to take the wheat from their storehouses where it is rotting and to give some air to the sugar and soap that the hoarders hide in their basements in order to sell them later at the price of gold.

Bread, goddammit! This is the watchword of the day. The sans-culottes don't envy the gods of the earth. They could give a fuck about their palaces, their cooks, their carriages, their horses, and their lackeys. Happiness isn't found in all this foolishness, but in labor and virtue. The sans-culottes know and desire no other. But the sans-culottes also need bread. The earth was made for all living creatures, and from the ant to the prideful insect called man, everyone must find his subsistence in the products of that common mother. I know that the big always want to swallow the little: wolves devour sheep, eagles tear out the guts of the timid turtledove. Man, for his part, destroys all, ravages all, eats everything that falls into his hands. There is not a single two-footed animal who hasn't eaten thousands of other animals over the course of his lifetime. The lions we look on as ferocious beasts, the tigers we only speak of with a shiver, are a thousand times less voracious than we. These savage and bloodthirsty beasts at least respect their kind and don't eat each other, but men have no more cruel enemies than themselves. They betray each other, they insult each other, they devour each other, they invent all kinds of methods to harm and destroy each other. And yet they boast of being nature's masterpiece and the image of the divinity. Fuck, what blasphemy! There's a strong chance the world wouldn't exist if its author were as wicked and cruel as man.

Whence, then, this dark humor, old babbler? What misfortune has befallen you, joyous furnace merchant? You who usually laugh at the stupidity of others and who are never as funny as when you want to get angry, what's gotten into you today? What grass did you walk on? Do you think you're worth more than your kind, you who speak with so much scorn? I don't scorn them, goddammit, I feel for them. What do you expect, when from north to south I hear the cannons rumble, when I see cities set aflame, the countryside ravaged, the earth covered in corpses. Am I not right to feel down? When I ask myself the cause of all these disorders and I think that a half dozen imbeciles called kings and emperors are the cause for all these ills I de-baptize myself, I smash my pipe, I tear out the hairs of my mustache, I beat everything around me, not even sparing my poor country girl. I fight with her over nothing. I get mad about the point of a needle. In a word, I'm the gloomiest bugger in the republic.

What heats up my bile even more, goddammit, is to see the French going at each other like cats and dogs and eating each other up instead of working hand in hand to drive out the brigands who are making war on them. The rich think only of their interests. The republic has no greater enemy than them. They detest the Revolution because it established liberty and equality. They want, no matter what, no matter how, to put themselves in the place of the big shots in order to rule over us and oppress the sans-culottes. They amass land on land; their cellars are full of our coins that they've buried there; every day they build their fortune on public ruin; they hoard all our foodstuffs; they brag of reducing us to misery if we don't reestablish royalty. The scumbags have in their hands all subsistence goods, prevent them from circulating, and they only take the wheat from their storehouses when it's rotten. And even then they charge us an arm and a leg for it.

Fuck! We have to put an end to this. It was proposed to the sans-culottes that there be a *levée en masse*. This is a good idea, but it's not against the Prussians, the Austrians, or the Spaniards that they should march. We have under arms nearly seven hundred thousand brave buggers who'll know how to rout the vile slaves who fight for the tyrants and make them bite the dust. Let our armies be delivered from the whole canaille of the ancien régime, from all the snobs with their red heels who've poisoned them. Never ceased to demand, let them be commanded by good old invalids and I guarantee you their success. We have in the interior enemies a thousand times more fearsome, and we'll never have rest as long as they exist. And so, goddammit, since they want all the republicans to march, it should only be against the traitors, the conspirators, and the hoarders who disturb and sap us from within. Mortal war on all the scoundrels. It won't last long of we are well led. Let there be formed in every department a corps of ten thousand sans-culottes paid by the republic. No need to spend a lot for their equipment and arms. The service they'll be charged with will not be difficult. Let them first take a stroll in the countryside to make the big farmers give an accounting of their harvest. After having left each canton a year's worth of provisions the rest should be transported to a common granary in each department after having been paid for, as is only right, from the public treasury. It is there, goddammit, that the armies and the big cities will find their subsistence goods, and since the year is good and the harvest can feed all the inhabitants of the republic for three years, there will be a reserve in case of scarcity.

After this operation, which will reestablish calm and dissipate all fears, our patriots will pay the same type of visit to the hoarders of Marseille, Lyon, Bordeaux, Nantes, and Rouen. Their storehouses will be emptied, and the sugar and soap that rot in the cellars where the fucking thieves have piled them up will get some air. We'll force them to sell them, and the abundance of these goods will cause their price to go down and all will be well, goddammit!

Yes, the rich only oppress us because we allow them to. Yes, goddammit, once we've decided to give sign of life all the crooked bankers and merchants will be forced to throw in the towel. They've hoarded our basic foods, so let us hoard hands to force them to surrender them to us. They'll have no choice but to surrender to force and, above all, the law. The merchant should live off his industry, and nothing could be fairer. But he shouldn't grow fat on the blood of the unfortunate. The most basic property is existence, and one must eat at whatever cost. Hunger draws the wolf from the woods. And so tremble, you bloodsuckers of the people. You wanted to reduce us to despair. You boasted that the sans-culottes would fall at your feet to beg you to give them a miserable piece of bread. The same arms that brought down the throne of the cuckold Capet will fall on you. You'll no longer thumb your noses at the decrees of the National Convention. You'll no longer insult the public misery. The people, your master, will not languish any longer. You reduced them to despair; they will strike. Quiver, goddammit!

■ THE GREAT JOY OF PÈRE DUCHESNE

1793

The great joy of Père Duchesne after having seen Marat in a dream, in which he made know to him all the schemers, thieves, and traitors who want to destroy the republic. Their patriotic fucking discussion on the means of saving the sans-culotterie. The vow of the old furnace merchant to always follow the path of the Friend of the People, despite the daggers and the poison of the statesmen.

I've been all fucked up since the death of Marat. Yes, dammit, ever since the Friend of the People is no more, sorrow is painted on the faces of the sans-culottes and joy reigns on the papier-mâché faces of all the escapees of Koblenz. When meeting, patriots cry and moan: we no longer have a guide, they say, we are like blind men who have lost their canes. While Marat lived we could sleep in peace, for he ceaselessly watched over us; he knew all the traitors and he pursued them wherever they were. Their most secret actions were known to him, and they couldn't cook up any low blows against the republic without our being warned of it. On their side the aristocrats bless the sacrilegious hand of the infamous Charlotte; they call her the Judith of the Calvados. Her knife, they say, was more useful to us than all the sabers, all the bayonets, and all the cannons of Prussia and Austria; from now on we can conspire without fear; we're rid of the cursed Argus who spied out all our actions and never ceased denouncing us.

All of these thoughts trouble my brain, and the memory of Marat follows me without end. Last night I saw him in a dream: his wound was still bleeding, dammit. Upon seeing it I cried. Friend of the People, I shouted, is it you? Yes, good Père Duchesne, it's Marat who comes from the dead to talk with you, because—dammit—the love of freedom pursues me even beyond the grave. Content to have lost my life for my republic, there only remains to me the regret of not having seen it delivered, before my death, from all the scoundrels who tear away at its breast. Père Duchesne, you must do what I couldn't do. You closely followed me in the Revolution; like me you consecrated your life to the defense of the rights of the people. You speak the language of the sans-culottes, and your foul mouth, which makes little mistresses faint, sounds beautiful to free men, for free men shouldn't be sought among the beautiful souls. Your joy and your anger have done more than all the dreams of statesmen. They know this well, the worthless fucks, and that's why they've persecuted you like they did me. Courage, old man; don't back off when you suffer the same trials as me. Don't be afraid: Is there a more beautiful death than mine? But since you're useful to your fellow citizens, try to avoid the daggers of statesmen. Live a while longer in order to denounce them and to complete, if you can, the task I'd undertaken.

Friend of the People, I said to him, I'm not fucking lacking in will; you remember what I said to you on the eve of your death upon seeing you worn out by work: I wanted to share with you my strength and my good health. I have enough, you said, to confound the schemers, as I did the statesmen. There are still a few in the Convention, there are even some of the Mountain, who I'd unmask. Yes, when

I can drag myself there I'll again be put under accusation, but the swindlers will be known. These, Marat, were the last words you addressed to me while shaking my hand: they are etched in my memory, dammit, and they'll never leave it.

Yes, Père Duchesne, you have to go after them hammer and tong, and not take it easy on anyone. When three months ago I proposed planting three hundred nooses on the terrace of the Tuileries in order to hang the perfidious representatives of the people there, some took me for a madman and others as someone thirsty for blood. But nevertheless, if I'd been believed, how much bloodshed would have been avoided! More than a million fewer men would have perished! So when I made that proposition I wasn't speaking as a bloody monster: on the contrary, I spoke as a friend of humanity. The moderates have buried more victims than those that fell before the steel of our enemies. Nothing is more harmful in a revolution than half measures. We have finally arrived at the era when we must pare things right down to the bone. The conspirators— whose numbers we stupidly allowed to increase—are on one side, and the patriots on the other. The combat has begun, but it is a combat unto death. No more quarter for the defeated party, because, fuck!, if the statesmen had the upper hand for one moment there wouldn't exist a single patriot in six months. The scoundrels have just proved what they are capable of. In Marseilles all the Jacobins were massacred; in Lyon more than a hundred republicans were guillotined by the royalists, the blood of the friends of freedom now flood the streets of Avignon. The statesmen wanted to begin a similar butchery in Paris when they had us arrested—you and I, Père Duchesne—but the worthless bastards don't know the sans-culottes of our faubourgs. Such horrors can't be committed among the men of July 14 and August 10. And so the statesmen have redirected their batteries! Having been able neither to corrupt nor shake the formidable mass of sans-culottes of Paris, they slandered them in all the departments; they presented them as ferocious beasts that only live off human flesh. The women of the Calvados, Finistère, and the Gironde, because of all these lies, scared their children by speaking to them about the ogre Marat, who had become more frightening to imbeciles than a werewolf; but posterity will judge me, Père Duchesne. It will know that he who was so many times accused of being ferocious was the best of humans, that he owned nothing, that he shared the fruit of his waking hours and his labors with the unfortunate, and that he left no other heritage but the good that he did for his fellows. But enough talk about me, let's think only of the republic.

You have just done something worthy of me by denouncing Custine. You have brought his plots and treason into broad daylight. If we had waited a few more days to recall him freedom would have been fucked. This infamous rascal, after having had the French in Frankfurt massacred, after having abandoned Mainz, after having allowed Valenciennes to be encircled, after having delivered Condé, only waited for the right moment to lead his army into a slaughter and to deliver the coup de grâce to the republic by sacrificing its last resources. Fortunately, the bugger has been put to the side. His crimes have been proved, let his head promptly fall under the national razor, but let his not be the only one! Let all the scoundrels who compose his headquarters also be shortened. Pursue, denounce without rest the infamous Tourville, who was the right arm of Lameth, and who will deliver Maubeuge if we leave him in command. Make known the swindler Lapallière, and especially the *ci-devant* marquis de Verigni, known in all the gaming houses under the name of

Debrulis. Tell the sans-culottes in the army that this rat has emigrated twice. Don't forget Leveneur, the intimate friend of Lafayette, and the henchman of Custine. Don't allow these bandits a moments rest until they've been chased and punished as traitors.[1]

Marat, I will profit from your lessons; fuck, yes, beloved shade, inspire me. I swear to you to brave daggers and poison and to always follow your example. Eternal war on conspirators, intriguers, and rogues, this is my motto, dammit. That was mine too, the ghost said to me while slipping away. Keep you word. Fuck, yes, I will keep it.

From *Le Père Duchesne*, no. 264, 1793.

---

1 Charles Tourville (1740–1809)—counterrevolutionary general; Theodore Lameth (1756–1854)—right-wing deputy on the Legislative Assembly, opponent of war with Austria. Fled to Switzerland when his arrest was ordered; Alexis Leveneur de Tillières (1746–1833)—general under Lafayette and Dumouriez, participant in the Battle of Valmy. Arrested twice as a noble.

■ J.R. HÉBERT, DEPUTY PROCURATOR OF THE COMMUNE

to his Fellow Citizens
Monday, May 27 of the second year of the Republic [1793][1]

I had resolved to preserve a profound silence concerning my arrest in order to deprive the counterrevolutionaries who wish to destroy me of any pretext for imputing to me the commotion they seek to incite in Paris. But since the most slanderous rumors are being spread about my detention it is my duty to destroy them and inform patriots of all the dangers that threaten them.

On Friday the 24th of this month, at the general council of the Commune, I was fulfilling the functions with which my fellow citizens honored me. At 9:00 p.m. a gendarme presented me with a summons from the Committee of the Twelve ordering me to immediately appear before them. I informed my colleagues of this and reminded them of their

---

1   On May 24, 1793, the moderates of the Commission of the Twelve ordered Hébert arrested for conspiratorial activities. He was released three days later, backed by the loyal sans-culottes, whose voice he was. Of the names mentioned in this piece, almost all were executed: Roland, Madame Roland, Brissot, Gorsas, Barbaroux, and Hébert himself in 1794. Pétion, a Robespierrist, committed suicide before he could be guillotined.

commitment to consider themselves as having been struck if any individual from among them was victim of an arbitrary act. After insisting on my innocence and telling my fellow citizens to protect themselves against the dangers threatening freedom, filled with the testimonies of esteem and friendship of all my colleagues, I followed the guard and went to the Duodecimvirs.

Starving wolves who prowl and growl while awaiting their prey are less impatient than the grand inquisitors were to see me arrive at their fearsome tribunal. My name resounded throughout the streets around the lair where my irons were being forged: "Is it the deputy procurator of the Commune? Is it Hébert? Is it Père Duchesne?"

There he was. At this word joy was painted on all their faces. The *virtuous* Pétion and the *honest* Barbaroux, who, enticed by the pleasure of reveling in my humiliation, wanted to join in the fun, were going to sit with this committee, but reading in my face the feelings their presence inspired in me, foreseeing all that I was going to say about them, they preferred leaving to announce the good news to their henchmen to remaining to witness the scene I am about to describe.

President Molvaux, after a few questions concerning my name, civil status, address, and the preliminary formalities, asked me if I was the author of a paper called *Père Duchesne*. "There's 'Père Duchesne' and there's 'Père Duchesne,'" I answered. "If you're talking about the player of false notes, if you're talking about those terribly patriotic letters that praised Lafayette to the heavens, that sang of the goodness of the last of our tyrants, that praised the virtues of the great Roland and the chaste spouse of that worthy minister, well I have nothing to do with that Père Duchesne. But if you mean that honest and loyal Père Duchesne who has pursued the traitors since the first days of the Revolution, I admit to being that one.

With a benign hand President Molvaux presented me the last six issues. After having read and examined them I recognized my work, with the exception of a few marginal notes and a few notes between the lines that I believe were written by messieurs Brissot and Gorsas.

Q: What was your intention in writing these abominable articles?

A: *They were written with the intention, gentlemen, of enlightening that interesting portion of the people that has always been disdained by refined spirits and for whom they never wrote. I thought that in speaking the language closest to nature, in swearing along with those who swear, I could teach important truths to honest citizens who only need a little bit of education to raise themselves to the highest virtues and to defend their rights.*

Q: What do you mean by "Brissotins" and "Girondins"?

A: *I already told you that having appropriated the vulgar tongue I had to use the expressions familiar to the sans-culottes. Don't you know that when in the produce markets they speak of a Brissotin or a Girondin it's as if they were speaking of a Dumouriez?*

Q: But you seem to be designating the Convention by these brazen expressions.

A: *Me, insult the Convention? If it were possible for it to be Brissotized and Rolandized the counterrevolution would have been carried out.*

Q: But you preach murder and carnage. You say in one of your papers that we must lay hands on the traitors.

A: *That's true, citizen inquisitors, and may it please heaven that all conspirators be choked.*

Q: But you say that if there were three hundred fewer rascals France would be saved.

A: *You see, citizen inquisitors, that I am moderate. Someone else would perhaps rightly say that more than three hundred thousand heads must fall in order to save freedom.*

Q: But you preach murder and anarchy; you want the Convention to be dissolved.

A: *Citizen inquisitors, it's no longer Père Duchesne who will speak, it's the people's magistrate who will answer you. Examine my private and political lives and you will see if I am a good man and a true patriot. Ask my colleagues of the Commune of August 10. Question the people, who have seen me constantly defend its rights and fulfill—if I may be allowed to say so— with dignity the position they've confided to me, and if you have any shame you'll blush at having dared suspect me of such crimes. You will learn that in all the counterrevolutionary movements that have occurred since last September I have always thrown myself into the crowd, I've spoken to the people in the language of a magistrate, and you'll learn that it is I, yes I, who put an end to the sugar conspiracy. You'll learn that on March 10 I denounced the undertakings that a handful of individuals wanted to allow themselves against several members of the Convention; that it was in accordance with my plea that all the security measures were taken. If in that case the Convention decreed that the municipality had deserved well of the republic, know that I had my part to play in that decree.*

After all these facts, whose delirious mind could think that I was a disorganizer, a conspirator against the national representation? Even if I've pronounced some erroneous opinions in my speeches and writings (which can't be proven), do you have the right to make a crime of this? Does the freedom of the press no longer exist? Do you alone have the right to speak all the foolishness imaginable and to vomit up the most disgusting slanders against patriots? If you are looking for disorganizers and anarchists, go find them in the shops of

your friends Brissot and Gorsas, whose pestilential produc-
tions have disseminated the germs of the war of the Vendée
and the civil war they want to start between Paris and the
departments.

Despite these categorical reasonings and responses, after
an interrogation of seven hours, I was transferred to the
prison de l'Abbaye, though I've not yet heard speak of an
interrogation, despite the fact that the law prescribes the
interrogation of every detainee within twenty-four hours
of his arrest. I have some quite sweet consolations in my
captivity. What a happy, what an honorable persecution.
What commitments I've made to the good citizens who
have come to visit me and bathe my irons with their tears.
Oh my Fatherland, you shall be saved! There exist too
many patriots for liberty to perish.

Brave sans-culottes, gather in all your sections. Loudly
demand the abolition of this committee of inquisition that
wants to destroy the Convention by exercising the most
tyrannical acts in its name. Over the course of the last night
the residents and secretaries of the section of the Cité were
torn from their wives' arms. One of them is national com-
missar for the tribunal of the sixth arrondissement and
cannot participate in today's hearing. You thus see that
the course of justice is interrupted, that the magistracy
is degraded, that the people's sovereignty is insulted and
ignored, that all powers are usurped, that the proscription
lists have been drawn up, that individual liberty no longer
exists, and that those of the press and opinion are oblit-
erated. What were you before July 14? What are you now?

Hébert, member of the commune of August 10, elector of the
department of Paris, deputy procurator of the commune.

SYLVAIN MARÉCHAL (1750–1803)

■ THE FESTIVAL OF REASON

An opera in one act
Performed by the National Opera on sextidi of the first decade of
Nivose, the second year of the Republic [1793][1]

Scene One
(Lisis, the mayor)

LISIS: Everything announces a calm day worthy of the
festival.
MAYOR: My son! We don't have much time. Have you
taken care of everything?
LISIS: The girls of the hamlet advance;
we have been preparing,
we have been awake since before the dawn,
and our elders have been asked to select the fairest face
to represent Reason,
and I hope that their votes will crown the tenderhearted
Alison.
SONG: My father, can you conceive
the drunkenness of my heart
if my tender shepherdess

---

1   A month after the large-scale Festival of Reason, when Notre
    Dame Cathedral was reconsecrated to Reason as part of the
    dechristianization campaign, Maréchal's opera, with music by
    the most important of revolutionary composers, André Grétry,
    was performed at the Opéra National.

were to have the honors of the day.
Yes, love owes this price to my patriotism.
From its lessons I've taken much;
enemy of all tyranny,
I adore liberty.
My father, can you conceive . . .

Scene Two
(*the preceding actors and a municipal officer*)

MUNICIPAL OFFICER: Friend, this is a great step
we are about to take.
But if to the necessary heights
the citizens are not . . .
MAYOR: We will set them on the march. . . . We have too
long been silent
MUNICIPAL OFFICER: Perhaps the people still need charlatans;
sacred prejudices still have their partisans
who mutter softly in the shadow of the mysteries.
DUET: (*the mayor and the municipal officer*)
OFFICER: Perhaps the people still need charlatans.
MAYOR: No, no, prejudices no longer have any partisans.
OFFICER: They'll softly speak in the shadow of the mysteries.
MAYOR: They'll speak so softly that it will be the same as
being silent.
MAYOR: The time has come! Let us break the unworthy
bond that has held the spirit in a shameful delirium.
The moment has come to dare everything, to say everything.
No, no, error serves no good.
OFFICER: Tell me, what will we put in place of priests?
MAYOR: Good magistrates who aren't liars.
OFFICER: And in the place of the gods so feared by our
ancestors?
MAYOR: Wise laws, good morals. . . .

Our hearts will render us masters of opinion.
Let us tear away the blindfold
that the people insist on keeping;
take the axe or the flame
to the root,
and smash the playthings
that wound the hands of childhood.
OFFICER: The fanaticism that we offend
will allow itself all evil deeds.
Fear all from the priest that we unmask. You know
that he is skilled at avenging himself.
MAYOR: I am at peace.
In order to fortify freedom
I would give my blood, my whole existence.
I want to give my life as well for the defense
of august truth.
TRIO: (*the mayor, his son, the municipal officer*)
Against fanaticism,
against despotism,
we swear to league together.
Holy truth,
holy liberty,
we three swear
to make their laws triumph
within these city walls
or all three to perish.
MAYOR (*to his son*): But let nothing transpire:
we must maintain secrecy until the prescribed moment.
LISIS: Our priest doesn't know what to say about all this.
Don't dread the indiscreet.

Scene III

MAYOR: Approach, young Citizen maidens,
to celebrate Reason's Day.

This festival is right for republicans. . . .
Elders, give us the name of the wisest one.
THE OLDEST OF THE ELDERS: Citizens, listen well . . . Modest Alison,
who three years ago lost her mother,
Alison fulfills this role for her whole family.
She is the support of her father,
and in her household
makes order, peace, the morality of the ancients,
and patriotic virtues reign. . . .
Appear, wise and beautiful Alison,
and serve this day as the emblem of Reason.
CHORUS OF VILLAGE WOMEN (softly): We all render homage to her virtues
despite her modest refusal.
The whole village proclaims her the wisest.
We all render homage to her virtues.
MAYOR: It is for Alison, kind companions,
nascent flowers of our fields!
Go prepare in silence
for the new festival
that the village, faithful to virtue,
shall celebrate.

Scene IV

LISIS (song): Alison has the prize. How sweet it is to me
to adore Reason under the charm of her graces!
Tender object of my heart! Ah, how sweet it is to me
to see
that in attaching myself to your steps
I still find myself on the path of duty!
Alison has the prize. How sweet it is to me
to adore Reason under the charm of her grace!
On all sides people are going to church,

mothers arrive walking slowly.
Let us go enjoy their surprise
at the spectacle that awaits them.

Scene V

(*The Village Mothers*)

A WOMAN: Neighbor! The door is closed. . . .
ANOTHER WOMAN: Yet today is Sunday.
ANOTHER WOMAN (*looking at the clock*): And it's the usual hour.
ANOTHER: Our priest has fallen back to sleep.
CHORUS: Knock on the door.
Mister priest,
are you sleeping?
Open the church, then! Are you an émigré?
A WOMAN: He doesn't answer. Who will say the mass?
ANOTHER: Today is our day to recite it.
ANOTHER: I who today at confession wanted . . .
CHORUS: Our pastor, are you deaf?
ANOTHER: Perhaps he's at the festival,
announced with the sound of the drum,
and that our young people have been preparing since
yesterday.
But why delay the divine service?
Where did he leave us the keys to the sacristy?
A WOMAN: Our priest has become like others, rather.
While waiting, let us now say the Our Father.
CHORUS (*softly*): Pater . . . Ave . . . Credo . . . Confiteor . . .
Lumen
Heal us of our burns St. Lawrence, first deacon,
and you, St. Fiacre, *ora pro nobis. Amen.*
CHORUS: Protect us, great St. Denis,
patron of the girls of Paris,
fulfill our wishes good St. Crispin,

protect us great St. Martin.
Oh great Saint. Come, oh you
who heals all.
(*the young girls of the village, preceded by Alison accompanied
by the elders and the municipal officers, arrive in order and sing*)

Scene VI

(*The entrance of the church opens or rather disappears to make
room for an altar placed on the former one. On the frontispiece can
be read*: to Reason)

Hymn to Reason
Divinity of all ages.
You who we adore without blushing.
Reason! You who our unwise ancestors
made moan under the yoke of error for years.
Be the guide of our fields,
purge them of all abuse,
inspire in the breast of our comrades,
the love of order and virtue.
ONE OF THE WOMEN (*astonished*): Neighbor! . . . Is it a
dream? . . . And what? . . .
to Reason? But I don't know any saints by that name. . . .
ANOTHER WOMAN: Of this hamlet St. Anne is the patron saint.
It is no longer she who is crowned!
What does all this mean?
Oh! God will punish us.

Second verse of the hymn
Make disappear from earth
all superstitions.
Impress your holy character
wherever the sun introduces its rays.
Curse of tyrants and priests,

you, sister of liberty,
Reason! On our country-style altars
claim your rights and your pride.
A WOMAN: None of this is in my book.
I think the town is drunk.

Third verse
The gifts of kind nature
under your eyes are better assigned.
The labor of the fields
through you from routine has been freed.
It's you who makes happy homes.
Take our children as soon as they're in their cradles.
May they all be wise republicans,
intrepid and triumphant!
A WOMAN: My God, my God,
in the holy place! . . .

Scene VII

THE PRIEST (*he arrives in the middle of the festival*):
In the Temple of Reason
and under nature's eye
I come to join with you all
and renounce imposture.
(*he rips up his prayer book*)
Here they are, the playthings
of the world's infancy.
(*beneath his robe he is dressed as a sans-culotte*)
I tear it in two,
that which hid so many crimes.
I forever renounce the impure priesthood,
for too long have I borne the celestial hobbyhorse
(*the censer*).
For too long, wretched skullcap

have you degraded my dignity.
As a free and thinking man . . . admitted to this festival,
place on my head, Citizens,
the Liberty Bonnet!

First couplet
In the Temple of Reason,
before nature's eyes,
I have come to join with you all
to abjure imposture
THE OLD WOMEN: Oh, my God! What is this?
Why this?
THE PRIEST: Yes, I am claiming my dignity
as a free and thinking man. At this festival I want placed
on my head
the Liberty Bonnet.
To the devil with the skullcap,
to the devil with the hobbyhorse,
I am now a sans-culotte (*repeat*)
CHORUS OF VILLAGERS: A sans-culotte priest! . . . (*repeat*)
The priest's second couplet
In order for us all to be as one
I want to go to Rome
to preach Reason to the Pope
and convert the holy man. . . .
Leave there the playthings
of the world's infancy;
tear up this cloth,
this dreadful priestly robe.
Claim your dignity
as a free and thinking man.
Take part too in the festival,
and place on your head
the Liberty Bonnet.

To the devil your skullcap,
to the devil your hobbyhorse,
me, I'll make you a sans-culotte,
I'll make you a sans-culotte.
CHORUS: A sans-culotte pope,
a sans-culotte pope.
MAYOR (*stopping some villagers who have already put a red
bonnet on the priest*):
A priest is always a priest. We would love, nevertheless,
to believe
that the vow of his mouth has been dictated by his heart.
(*to the priest*)
It is up to you now to put the lie to history.
Consecrate the future to being deserving of the honor,
through civic conduct
of being the adopted child of our republic.
General Chorus (*of the entire hamlet, burning on the Altar of
Reason the prayer books, crosses, ornaments, etc.*):
Good morals, wise laws!
No more priests, no more kings.
MAYOR: You, good mothers of families,
see them! These are your daughters
who from here on, through their virtues,
will replace all your worm-eaten saints.
Forget your past errors.
To Reason finally raise
your thoughts.
Let all be as one.
GENERAL CHORUS: No more priests, no more kings.
Good morals, wise laws.
No more priests, no more kings!

■ THE CATECHISM OF THE CURÉ MESLIER

About all his prejudices, man is ready to blush.
His long infancy, he is ready to leave behind.
He tires of his yoke, he moves, he murmurs,
He dares to call on Nature's rights. . . .
Finally, the people think . . .
Nil credo auguribus, qui aures verbis devitant
Alienas, suas ut auro locupletant domos.
Soothsayers, chase from me all these charlatans
Who sell words devoid of meaning at a great price.

The editor in good faith to readers of good intentions:

This book is not an attack. Neither slanders, nor calumnies, nor personal attacks will be found here. For a long time the friends of order and truth have been whispering what we dare to write and publish here.

Error and falsehood had their moment of usefulness and served as a brake on an enslaved and ignorant people. But from the moment when a nation becomes enlightened and free it both should and can only be governed by its own laws. When a temple is built its scaffolding becomes useless and harmful: it is taken down. Having reached the age of reason we reject the playthings of childhood. All we now need are public virtues and private morality.

N.B.: There are certain prejudices that must be attacked, and which can only be destroyed with the arm of ridicule.

Epitaph of the Curé Meslier

> *here lies jean meslier*
> *curate of etrepigni, a village in the champagne*
> *died in 1733*
> *at the age of fifty-five*
> *upon his death he retracted*
> *that which he preached during his life*
> *and*
> *had no need to believe in god*
> *to be an honest man*

Catechism of the Curé Meslier

I. On God

Q: What is God?

A: *God is whatever the priests want.*

Q: Why is it said that he is a spirit?

A: *To frighten those who are entirely made up of matter.*

Q: Why eternal?

A: *In order to make the Church's power last longer.*

Q: Why independent?

A: *Because the priests have never wanted to depend on anyone.*

Q: Why infinite?

A: *Because the Church wants to have no limits.*

Q: Why omnipresent?

A: *Because the priests have need of him everywhere.*

Q: Why omnipotent?

A: *He is omnipotent as long as we believe him to be so.*

Q: What does it mean that he has created everything?

A: *It doesn't mean anything.*

Q: Why did God create us and put us on earth?

A: *So we could fear him and serve him in the person of his priests.*

II. On the Trinity

Q: Are there several gods?

A: *Yes and no. There is only one God, but this unique God makes three.*

Q: Why are these three divine personages equal in all things?

A: *So that the priests can have three strings to their bows.*

Q: What should be concluded from the mysteries of the Holy Trinity?

A: *That it is a renewed dream of the Greeks. See Plato, etc.*

III. On the Incarnation

Q: What does "a God made man" mean?

A: *It means that a man wanted to pass for God*

Q: Is he in fact God and man, both together?

A: *There is no answer to such a foolish question.*

IV. The Symbol

Q: Tell us your Credo.

A: *I believe only in virtue. If a God exists, I don't believe he had a son and that this son was hung and that he will one day come to judge the living and the dead. I don't believe in the Holy Spirit of the Church either, and even less in its infallibility. I would very much like to persuade myself that there is a resurrection of the flesh, and I would quite like there to be eternal life.*

Q: Explain those first words: "I believe only in virtue."

A: *Because virtue seems to me to be the only divinity worthy of the heart of man.*

Q: Why do you say: "If a God exists"?

A: *That is to say, I don't dare affirm the existence of a God since I see evil and evildoers on earth, and I'd rather deny the existence of a God than make a tyrant of him.*

Q: What do you mean by the words: "I don't believe he had a son"?

A: *Because God the Father and God the Son seem to me to be indecent and ridiculous.*

Q: Why don't you believe in the Holy Spirit?

A: *Because I don't understand a thing of this pious nonsense.*

Q: Why do you add: "And even less in the infallibility of the Church"?

A: *Because he who deceives can be deceived.*

Q: What do you mean by "the resurrection of the flesh"?

A: *I mean absurdity. The resurrection of the body is nothing but a trap laid for those who have no intelligence.*

Q: Why do you appear to desire more than hope for a life to come?

A: *Because a good and omnipotent father should have put his children in the best of all possible worlds.*

V. On the Sacraments in General

Q: What are the sacraments in general?

A: *They are superstitious practices instituted by the deceitful in order to lead the foolish.*

Q: Why does the Church make use of so many ceremonies in the administration of the sacraments?

A: *Because it knows the human heart. Because it isn't ignorant of the people's need for spectacles. Because your sprits are led when your senses are struck.*

VI. On Baptism

Q: What is baptism?

A: *It is a little bath given to children who have just been born and who are already guilty, it is said, of a terrible sin committed thousands of years ago by our first ancestors.*

Q: Does baptism wipe away all sins?

A: *Yes! A man who would prudently wait for the moment of his death to have himself baptized could conduct himself ad libitum during his life. Baptism would wash him of his worst filth. This is quite convenient.*

Q: Can baptism be supplemented?

A: *Yes, by having someone else slaughter or by carrying out slaughter oneself in order to defend the interests of the peaceful religion. This is what is called baptism by blood. The St. Bartholomew's Day expedition was a baptism by blood. The Inquisition is a baptism by fire.*

VII. On Confirmation

Q: What is confirmation?

A: *It's a kind of spiritual accolade given to you by the Church, and by which you become its faithful knight in all circumstances.*

Q: What are the effects of the sacrament of confirmation?

A: *In the first place, it makes us perfect Christians—stubborn and intolerant, tough fathers, gruff husbands, and citizens without a country. Next, it doesn't give us intelligence. Rather it gives us Holy Spirit, which doesn't, as was the case in the time of the Apostles, carry out any more miracles by descending upon us in tongues of fire but inhabits us incognito. In the third place, it renders us insensible, not to the threats of tyrants, for there are none any longer who persecute Christians but to the contempt of those philosophers who have found Christians to be persecutors in their turn.*

Q: What is Holy Oil?

A: *It is made up of oil and balm, emblems of the gentleness and good examples we have the right to demand of the prelates who confer this sacrament.*

Q: Why is a slap given?

A: *It's another emblem of the affronts and ill treatment that must be devoured in the service of these same prelates, who are not all Fénelons.*

Q: Is this sacrament absolutely necessary in order to be saved?

A: *The priests themselves admit that this is not the case.*

Q: On what occasion must we principally receive it?

A: *When we want to have our faith shaken. We have never had such need of this sacrament as today, and it has never been so neglected.*

Q: What disposition does this sacrament demand?

A: *A large provision of faith, blind devotion, and a head of bronze.*

VII. On the Eucharist

Q: What is the Eucharist?

A: *It's a round of the priest's goblets.*

Q: What is the word for the supposed changing of bread and wine?

A: *This switch is called transubstantiation, a big word that impresses the dim-witted.*

Q: How does this metamorphosis occur?

A: *This metamorphosis occurs by virtue of two or three lines of bad Latin gravely pronounced by a priest who is doubtless laughing up his sleeve all the while.*

Q: Isn't there only the body in the form of the bread and the blood in the form of the wine?

A: *God is there in his entirety under both forms and in his entirety in each part of these same forms in such a way that (in order to make this more easily understood via an example) if he breaks wind while the priest is saying mass the least zephyr disperses as many gods as crumbs of that divine dough. It flows from this that while barking or chasing down flies the little dog of the communicant shares in the communion with its mistress and of its mistress's almoner.*

Q: And what are the effects of the sacrament?

A: *In order to answer you again with a real event I will quote the bon mot of an unworthy Capuchin. He was almoner of one of the Queens of Spain, and a courtier having treated him in a cavalier fashion our Capuchin said to him with a feigned impudence: Know well that every day I have your Queen at my feet and your God in my hands.*

Q: And what must be our disposition when we receive the God bread?

A: *There are two kinds. One has to do with the soul, the other with the body.*

The first are: a foolish faith and the confession of your sins to a confessor. As for the second: one must not have eaten bread. One must, for fear of shaking one's faith, close one's eyes and swallow one's God without chewing. Jacques Clément, of blessed memory, still had his God on his lips when, armed with a dagger, imitating Judith, he bravely massacred his king.

Q: What crime is committed by those who take communion while in a state of mortal sin?

A: *They commit a sacrilege a thousand times more horrible than if they'd killed the good Henri or their father.*

IX. On the Mass

Q: What is the sacrifice of the mass?

A: *It's the daily bread of the priests.*

Q: Why was it instituted?

A: *In order to endlessly remind us that the Jews made a fanatic suffer who they should have sent out to the fields with the sheep of which he so often said he was the pastor or with the herd of pigs that that maniac frightened and drowned.*

Q: What must be one's state when assisting in this sacrifice?

A: *One must participate in the holy mass while thinking to oneself that it is not impossible to one day see the man who is leading the service in his bedroom before his chamber pot,* *for they have managed to have him render divine that which in a short while he must digest.*

X. On Penitence

Q: What is penitence?

A: *Of all of the sacraments that the Church has imagined, this one is its masterpiece. It can be defined as: the art of forcing the foolish to talk.*

Q: How many parts does it have?

A: *Three: contrition, confession, and satisfaction. It's mainly on the last two that the Church depends.*

Q: What is contrition?

A: *It's a feigned hatred for the sins we have committed, with the tacit promise of falling into it again the moment after.*

Q: What is confession?

A: *It's a shameful tribute that the Church raises on the timorous conscience of the credulous in order to have them do exactly what it wants, once it has learned their secrets.*

Q: Must one declare all one's sins?

A: *Well, what if we skipped one . . . ?*

Q: Is the confession of venal sins absolutely necessary?

A: *It's not exactly de rigueur, but it is nevertheless very useful . . . to priests. In this way they can study the spirit of a household and can then act in keeping with it.*

Q: What is satisfaction?

A: *It's a reparation owed to God, i.e., to his priests, for the injustices committed against one's neighbors.*

Q: What is absolution?

A: *It's an oral quittance that saves you from eternal punishment in the next life, but which doesn't absolve you (make note of this last article) of a temporal satisfaction in this life. It is here that your spiritual director lies in wait for you.*

Q: What are the works of penitence?

A: *It is to obey immediately and blindly all that is prescribed by the confessor. If the case were to arise, it is to act, for example, like the docile Cadière with the fortunate Girard. . . . See the causes célèbres, etc., etc., etc.*

XI. On Indulgences

Q: What is an indulgence?

A: *It's the Church's source of variable revenue. It's a sacred gag that one buys in order to prevent remorse from making one mad with its importuning cries.*

N.B. One must be careful not to confuse papal indulgences with philosopher's indulgences.

Q: By what power does the Church grant indulgences?

A: *By the powers transmitted to it through abuse and ignorance.*

Q: What must be done to earn indulgences?

A: *The conditions prescribed by the Church must be fulfilled, i.e., fill its trunks, kiss the priests' sandals, and sometimes do even worse, etc., etc., etc.*

XII. Extreme Unction and Last Rites

Q: What is this ceremony?

A: *It's a skillful method invented by the priests to take over the last moments of a sick person and to profit by the weakness of his mind in order to obtain from him all that the priest envied.*

Q: What are the effects of this?

A: *To frighten the moribund, to make him even sicker, and to have him insert into his will clauses that don't always please widows and orphans. Priests also say that this sacrament returns health to the body. But since a sick man, reduced to last rites, hardly ever returns, the Church has shrewdly added: if health is necessary for the salvation of the sick man. In this way, the Church makes itself responsible for nothing.*

XIII. On Orders

Q: What are orders?

A: *They the worst of all sacraments. They are that which give us spiritual tyrants, more fearful than the others. They are that which assure the most deceitful of men the right to do with impunity whatever they want in heaven's name.*

Q: Where does this power come from?

A: *From the barbarism of time, from prejudices, from false policies, from ambition, etc., etc.*

Q: How has this power come down to us?

A: *Alas, I don't know. It's perhaps because at all times there have been fools and deceivers on earth. We have been threatened that this despotism, all the more odious because it is sacred, will last until the end of time, per omnia saecula saeculorum. This is not the appropriate time to say: Amen.*

Q: With what disposition must one receive this sacrament?

A: *There are four principal dispositions for admission to ordination. They are: Impudence, Dissimulation, Ignorance, and a Heart of Stone.*

XIV. On Marriage

Q: What is marriage?

A: *This is a question that always makes me smile when I hear it proposed to a fifteen-year-old girl by a clerk of twenty.*

Q: What is the sacrament of marriage?

A: *It's a strange right that priests have always arrogated to themselves and that they maintain over pleasures that are forbidden them. Which proves that priests have to have their hands in everything. Let's be happy that they content themselves with blessing the nuptial bed without demanding a tithe!*

XVI. On God's Commandments

Q: In order to be saved is it enough to be baptized and have faith?

A: *No. One must keep God's commandments, and especially those of the Church.*

Q: What are God's commandments?

A: *With the exception of the first three, that Moses was careful enough to put at the head of the Decalogue because they have to do with priests, the seven following ones are nothing but the simplest laws, the elements of morality engraved in the hearts of all men, and that the most ancient and most skillful of the three imposters had no need to go and retrieve on a high mountain, nor to have them written on tablets of bronze by his God's finger.*

Q: Can you recite these commandments in French verse?

A: *You are quite generous in calling this verse; they are nothing but bad prose poorly rhymed.*

Q: What does it mean to believe in God?

A: *It means submitting in a servile fashion to all that the Church claims to have received from God through revelation.*

Q: How did God reveal himself?

A: *Through writings, a more than suspect monument, as well as through an uncertain tradition, and through infallible priests, though they are nothing but men.*

Q: How does one sin against the faith?

A: *In four ways:*
1. By using one's reason;
2. By daring to doubt;
3. By remaining neutral or indifferent;
4. By being tolerant.

Q: What does it mean to have hope in God?

A: *It means feeding oneself on chimeras.*

Q: How does one sin against hope in God?

A: *By not believing (perhaps not without reason) in providence, author at one and the same time of good and evil, and who makes the rain and the sunshine.*

Q: What does it mean to love God?

A: *It means doing the impossible, for who has ever been able to love that which he knows not, which he has never seen, and which he fears?*

Q: How does one sin against the love of God?

A: *By closing one's heart to a tyrant who allows second causes to act, who can at any moment obliterate me, as happened with the earthquake in Lisbon, etc., etc., etc.*

Q: Are we obliged to love our neighbor?

A: *Theologically speaking, we are only obliged to do so as long as the interests of priests don't suffer, for they are the first friends, the first parents, the first of the poor, etc.*

Q: What does it mean to adore God?

A: *It means groveling at the feet of his agents.*

Q: Can we pray to saints?

A: *Why not? Don't we obtain everything of a bishop when we have won away his mistress, or that of his grand vicar?*

Q: How should we invoke the saints?

A: *By filling their altars, served by priests, with rich offerings.*

Q: Don't we insult J C by praying to the saints?

A: *Not at all. They agree among themselves.*

Q: Can we honor the relics of saints?

A: *This is very much permitted to you. We are especially invited to cover them in riches.*

Q: Do we sin when we honor images?

A: *Not any more than the poor gentiles sinned who were treated as idolaters; while we will only be saved for the same reason we damn them.*

Q: What is Sunday?

A: *It's the day that the Almighty, who could have created a thousand worlds with one breath, rested after having much difficulty* *in finishing our miserable little planet. Even though it is said that there were three of them working at this difficult task.*

Q: Why does the Church sanctify Sunday?

A: *To make some money.*

Q: What must be done in order to sanctify Sunday?

A: *You have to be lazy, blurt out bad Latin that you don't understand, put something in the priest's plate, and sleep during his preaching or his sermon.*

Q: What do they do, those who sin against the sanctification of Sunday?

A: *All those who have too much of an ear to love plainchant and too much judgment to be content with the platitudes of a nasal Capuchin, or else those who feel they've wasted a day if they haven't consecrated it to some useful work.*

Q: What do God's other commandments oblige us to do?

A: *I would be insulting the children of man if I suspected them of needing to learn that which nature inspires in them at birth.*

XVI. On the Commandments of the Church

Q: Does the Church have the power to make commandments?

A: *At the very least there are spirits foolish enough to think so.*

Q: How many commandments of the Church are there?

A: *A half dozen.*

Q: What are the holidays instituted by the Church?

A: *There are two kinds. There are those having to do with the mysteries: these are the greatest and the most absurd. The others have as object the honoring of the Virgin and the saints. These are the most lucrative and the most numerous.*

Q: What is a saint?

A: *It's a man who has ceased to be one for his own torment and that of others.*

Q: What does the second commandment oblige us to do?

A: *To assist at all offices, both of the day and the night, i.e., to assiduously court the priests.*

Q: And the third?

A: *To confession. Cleanliness consists in purifying the body every day. The soul only needs this at least once a year.*

Q: With what punishment does the Church threaten those who don't fulfill the fourth?

A: *Entry into the temple is forbidden them during their lives and the sepulcher after their deaths.*

Q: What do the fifth and sixth commandments oblige you to do?

A: *To eat more but less often or later and to prefer a pike to your ordinary potage.*

Q: Why were fasting and abstinence instituted?

A: *Among other conjectures, this one is possible: during the Church's early days a bishop had ponds as his sole source of revenue. Consequently, he ordered the eating of fish throughout his diocese.*

XVII. On Sin

Q: What is original sin?

A: *An injustice worthy of Tiberius.*

Q: What is a capital sin?

A: *Since examples are within the reach of more people than definitions, I answer that philosophy is a capital sin since it gives birth to three mortal sins for which the Church still refuses absolution, to wit: incredulity, skepticism, and tolerance.*

Q: What is the opposite of philosophy?

A: *Theology, which is also divided into three branches, to wit: the love of prejudice, faith based on a word, fanaticism.*

Q: Where did the Church get the idea for seven moral capital sins?

A: *In its own bosom. In fact, there is nothing more prideful than a Capuchin, nothing more avaricious than a prelate, nothing* *more given to lust than a Carmelite, nothing more envious than a young priest, nothing more gluttonous than a nun, nothing more choleric than a pope, nothing lazier than a canon.*

XVIII. On the State of Man after His Death

Q: What becomes of man after his death?

A: *Whatever he becomes he is happy, since he is out of the hands of the priesthood.*

Q: What is the recompense God promises the just?

A: *It's getting to know if he resembles those who represent him on earth.*

Q: Do all the just see God after their deaths?

A: *No, only those fortunate enough to have seen their confessor before dying.*

Q: What does it mean to be one of the just?

A: *It's a good Christian for whom care was taken to pay for the presence of his priest at his funeral procession, who didn't forget to place under the chandelier the going price for a porte-dieu, and who gave a tip to the bell ringers who burst the eardrums of his neighbors and the apostolic crooks who laid him beneath the earth.*

Q: Why do we pray for the dead?

A: *To get money from the living.*

Q: What is purgatory?

A: *It's the brazier that boils the kettle of the pastor whose listeners furnish the wood.*

Q: What is the punishment of the evil?

A: *Their bodies suffer fire, their souls as well. Yes, their souls: the catechism assembled by order of Monsignor . . . says this, and I am nothing here but the copyist.*

XIX. On the Sign of the Cross

Q: Why do we make the sign of the cross?

A: *This sign is the rallying point, the war cry of Christians. At the St. Bartholomew's Day Massacre it served to distinguish the charitable Catholics who were piously murdering their Protestant fellow citizens.*

XX. On the Our Father and the Angelic Salutation

Q: What is the Sunday prayer?

A: *It's a prayer that certainly doesn't have a philosopher as its author, and even less a man of taste.*

Q: Say your "Our Father."

A: *I'm going to read it to you, for my recalcitrant memory has never been able to retain all of it.*

Q: Why do you say "Our Father"?

A: *To tell you the truth, I have no idea, since God doesn't treat us like his children.*

Q: Why do you say "Who art in heaven"?

A: *I say it this way because it is written this way, for I have for a long time seen in these few words a terrific inconsistency, and even a manifest contradiction. Isn't God everywhere?*

Q: Explain to us "May thy kingdom come."

A: *In fact, it's about time that the Master arrives, since we're beginning to tire of his valets.*

Q: And these words "Thy will be done."

A: *Seem ridiculous to me. The Catholics are the very first people who have taken it into their heads to tell their absolute master that they want to obey him.*

Q: "Give us this day our daily bread."

A: *If I were a father I would scold my children if they were to make up a prayer so injurious to my obligations and my heart.*

Q: Why do you say "Forgive us our transgressions"?

A: *I say this in order to obey you, for a man can no more anger a God than please him. In any event, in order to be just and clement, does God need us to remind him of his fairness and his goodness?*

Q: Explain "As we pardon those who have offended us."

A: *I always tremble when I hear this passage come out of the mouth of a priest. Alas, what would become of us if God didn't forgive any better than his ministers?*

Q: And "lead us not into temptation"?

A: *I find it repugnant to pronounce this article for I believe it to be a veritable blasphemy. What? A God who tempts man? Is God one with the devil? One would tend to believe it.*

Q: But "deliver us from evil."

A: *What evil?*

The Ave Maria

Q: What is the angelic salutation?

A: *It's a little Hebraic madrigal that the angel Gabriel composed on behalf of his master the Holy Spirit for the Virgin Mary, the wife of Joseph the carpenter. If I were a mother I would hesitate to have it learned, and especially to explain its meaning to my daughters.*

End of the categorical responses to the principal demands of the Paris catechism.

Second Part

Categorical responses to the principal demands of the Montpellier Catechism

Q: Give us an idea of the truths of religion.

A: *These truths aren't good to be told.*

Q: Into how many parts can we reduce all the truths of religion?

A: *There aren't enough to make a very thick volume.*

Q: Are we certain that there is a God?

A: *Not as much as of Euclidean geometry or the mathematics of Barème.*

Q: By what reasons can we convince ourselves that there is a God?

A: *It wouldn't be those that we can draw from physical and moral evil.*

Q: Why do the scriptures speak of the arms, the legs, the hands, the feet of God?

A: *Because if the monkeys made for themselves an image of God he would be as hairy as a monkey. The King of England, John the Landless, prayed by the teeth of God.*

Q: Is it not also said in these same Holy Scriptures that God became angry?

A: *Yes, to be sure, and in more than one place. Which proves that when we want to speak of that which we know nothing about we expose ourselves to many contradictions and inconsistencies.*

Q: Is there only one God?

A: *That question is hardly philosophical and doesn't deserve a response. The Church says that there is only one but at the same time it found in him enough material to make three if it is necessary. It made of this a polyp.*

Q: Isn't it unreasonable to believe what we don't understand?

A: *Who is saying the contrary?*

Q: Are we certain that God revealed the mystery of the Holy Trinity?

A: *As much as we can be of an absurdity.*

Q: How does God make Himself known outside of Himself?

A: *That's an enigma about which priests brag they have the key. They are bolder than philosophers.*

Q: What are God's works?

A: *If the priests are involved in this, and if we know the worker by his works, it must be admitted that that God hasn't always done good work.*

Q: Was it the Father, the Son, or the Holy Ghost who made the world?

A: *Three were hardly enough to get this done.*

Q: Why did God create the heavens and the earth?

A: *God doesn't have to render any accounts.*

Q: How did he make the heavens and the earth?

A: *The "how" is no easier to explain than the "why." We'll never finish if you ask the "hows" and "whys" of religion.*

Q: Did God create the heavens and the earth a long time ago?

A: *Some chronologists put him to work early and others later. Some, in order not to make mistakes in such difficult calculations, make the world eternal and thus cut the knot.*

Q: How much time did God employ in making the world?

A: *Barely a whole week.*

Q: What are angels?

A: *They are mixed beings, amphibian animals, half god, half man. They are commission agents of the old Eternal Father. One could take them for bad copies of the demigods of profane mythology.*

Q: Are angels naked or dressed?

A: *Joan of Arc's answer at her interrogation at Rouen: Do you think that God doesn't have what he needs to dress them?*

Q: What does eternal life consist in?

A: *When we get there we'll know.*

Q: What are demons?

A: *As Count Ruggeri said, demons are nothing but each man's enemies, and who doesn't have some?*

Q: Are all demons in hell?

A: *Alas, no. There are on earth male and female demons, domestic demons, political demons, ecclesiastical demons, and the latter are the worst of all.*

Q: What is hell?

A: *When we get there we'll know.*

Q: What is the most perfect creature?

A: *Man never fails to cry out: it's me!*

Q: How did God form man?

A: *Another "how"? But "how" can we ask this question?*

Q: What is the soul?

A: *When the mechanism of the body is fully explained to me I'll be able to tell you what the soul is.*

Q: What are the tree of life and the science of good and evil that Genesis speaks of?

A: *It's perhaps the emblem of a thing whose proper name would make a virgin blush.*

Q: How did the devil seduce Eve?

A: *The same way men have had their way since then with all the women who've been attacked.*

Q: What is the Flood?

A: *It wasn't the most beautiful of miracles of the Father of all mercies.*

Q: Who was Noah?

A: *Noah was the father of drunks, just as Adam was of cuckolds. One allowed himself to be mocked by his children, and the other allowed himself to have horns put on by his wife. Both of them models worthy of those who offer and of those to whom they are offered.*

Q: What does Noah's Ark mean in a figurative sense?

A: *Noah's Ark represents the Church.*

Q: What is the Tower of Babel (still figuratively).

A: *The Tower of Babel is yet again the symbol of the Church, where we speak without being understood and where ambition is limitless.*

Q: Who was Abraham?

A: *The father of believers. His family decreases daily and will soon be extinguished.*

Q: What is the sacrifice of Isaac?

A: *An atrocity. A mother has said on this subject that God would never have asked for such a sacrifice from a mother. A Jewess or a believer would nevertheless have been capable.*

Q: What did Joseph do with the wife of Potiphar?

A: *Nothing.*

Q: Who was Moses?

A: *The most skillful and the least fortunate of the three imposters.*

Q: What is the meaning of the Paschal lamb?

A: *Childish silliness. Some people have seen in it the conduct of priests who, dressed in the fleece of the lambs whose care has been confided to them, slaughter them in order to feed the flock of which they shamelessly call themselves the pastors, and of which they are nothing but the butchers.*

Q: What is the meaning of the crossing of the Red Sea?

A: *A miracle for the foolish, foolishness for sensible beings.*

Q: What is the meaning of the Mass?

A: *Idem.*

Q: What did Moses do on Mount Sinai?

A: *He made up a thousand drugs that would today find no purchasers.*

Q: How did David live?

A: *The same way that all libertine and tyrannical kings have lived since then.*

Q: How did Solomon live?

A: *See the Song of Songs.*

Q: What were the Prophets?

A: *Either rascals or fools.*

Q: What was Job?

A: *The image of many people.*

Q: What are prophecies?

A: *Sunt verba et voces, praetereaque nihil,*[1] *like ancient French music.*

Q: What was Jesus Christ?

A: *The putative son of a member of the carpenter's guild.*

Q: What was the Virgin?

A: *The putative wife of a carpenter.*

---

1 They are words and voices and nothing else. In other words, nonsense.

Q: Was she always a virgin?

A: *As much as one can be when one has had a child.*

Q: And St. Joseph, what was he?

A: *That which so many spouses still are who don't think they resemble him very much.*

Q: Why did Jesus Christ want to be born in a stable?

A: *The stable where he was born was a figure of his Church: the ox, the ass, the pastors, and the mulatto kings represent those who were one day to enter the Church's sphere.*

Q: What do we know about the childhood of Jesus Christ?

A: *Nothing, and to judge by what he did from his adolescence until his early death we don't lose much in not knowing.*

Q: What kind of life did Jesus Christ lead?

A: *A life that would earn him nothing today but a loge at lunatic asylum or a bed in a madhouse.*

Q: What did Jesus Christ do?

A: *Something we shouldn't take it into our heads to do ourselves. It cost him entirely too much.*

Q: What do you mean by the words "Jesus Christ was transfigured"?

A: *I mean a trick that wouldn't take anyone in today.*

Q: What is the Passion of Jesus Christ?

A: *The torture of a fanatic who was more to be pitied than blamed, and who deserved pity more than hatred.*

Q: What did Jesus Christ do on the cross?

A: *He rendered up his spirit, and this wasn't the most painful moment of his torture.*

Q: What were the miracles that occurred upon the death of Jesus Christ?

A: *The greatest of these miracles is that we still talk about this today.*

Q: Why did God want to die in so ignominious a fashion?

A: *We don't owe him as much gratitude as that. The kind of death he suffered was perhaps not his choice.*

Q: What benefits did Jesus Christ procure for us through his death?

A: *If only they were merely the St. Bartholomew's Day Massacre and the Holy Inquisition.*

Q: What do you mean when you say that Jesus Christ is dead?

A: *I mean a quite ordinary historical event.*

Q: Was Jesus Christ resuscitated?

A: *This is not a historical event. This question belongs to modern mythology that, parenthetically, is worth no more than the older version.*

Q: After the Resurrection, who did Jesus Christ show himself to?

A: *The first person he allowed to touch him was a woman.*

Q: Is Jesus Christ no longer on earth?

A: *The greatest part of him, his intolerance and fanaticism, is still here.*

Q: What place does Jesus Christ occupy in heaven?

A: *He is seated at the right hand of his father.*

Q: Does God have a right hand?

A: *Do you think he is armless? His substitutes at least aren't.*

Q: Why do you say that Jesus Christ is seated in heaven?

A: *Even a God cannot remain standing through all eternity.*

Q: Why do you say that God is our bread?

A: *Because we eat it at an inn, served by priests who reasonably ransom their invitees. There hardly exists a lighter or more expensive meal.*

Q: What are the things about Jesus Christ that we should imitate?

A: *I'd rather tell you those things we should forbid ourselves.*

Q: How did the Holy Spirit descend upon the Apostles?

A: *In tongues of fire. This is why, when their successors speak, they set everything ablaze.*

Q: What is a martyr?

A: *A man who has lost his head, or who never had one.*

Q: What is the Church?

A: *It's a flock of sheep led by wolves disguised as pastors.*

Q: What is the spirit that animates the body of the Church?

A: *It is up to ecclesiastical history to instruct us in this matter. Let us stop, for example, at the torture of Jan Hus.*

Q: What is a Christian?

A: *St. Justin Martyr will answer you for me: Omnes qui ratione vixere, sunt Christiani, etiamsi Athei.*

Q: Will the Church last until the end of the world?

A: *We are threatened with this, but we will appeal to the Tribunal of Reason.*

Q: What do you mean by the Roman Church?

A: *That which does the most harm and the least good, because it is the strongest.*

Q: Why is the bishop of Rome called the pope?

A: *It's a Greek word that means father. The popes have forgotten the etymology of their name, or rather never knew it.*

Q: Who are the enemies of religion?

A: *All the friends of Reason.*

Q: What are the advantages of religion?

A: *Only priests can answer this question.*

Q: Should Christians study the Holy Scriptures?

A: *I pity their faith if they pay too much attention to this.*

Q: Do all the Church's usages come from the Apostles?

A: *One must be fair: for their honor, not all of them do.*

Q: What is a council?

A: *In order to give a correct idea it would be appropriate to apply to a council the words of Piron on the Académie Française: "There are forty of them there, and they have the wit of four."*

Q: Is faith the same for all who believe?

A: *Some have a living faith, others a dead or dying one. And then there are those, and they are the majority, who have neither the one nor the other.*

Q: What is a vow?

A: *Ordinarily, it's a promise that we don't keep.*

Q: What is chastity?

A: *Ask a Carmelite monk.*

Q: What does it mean to tell a lie?

A: *It's acting like a Prophet.*

Q: Is it sometimes permitted to lie?

A: *A priest would tell you yes. An honest man would tell you no.*

Q: What is flattery?

A: *No one could better define this than the king's Confessor.*

Q: Is Jesus Christ a great name?

A: *I know holier ones.*

Q: Why did Jesus Christ enter Jerusalem on an ass?

A: *The stubborn and ignorant ass was the symbol of the future Church.*

Q: Why are bells not sounded from Thursday to Holy Saturday?

A: *In order to not awaken the sleeping cat.*

Q: Why are the offices of the Holy Week called Ténèbres [shadows]?

A: *It is true that we could give this name to the offices the Church celebrates all year long.*

Q: Why do we extinguish the lamps during the evening office of Holy Week?

A: *In order to allegorically show that the Church extinguishes in us the flame of truth.*

Q: Why do we make noise during these same offices?

A: *All of these ceremonies are the symbol of the conduct of the Holy Roman Apostolic Church and others.*

Q: Why do we strip altars bare?

A: *In order to exhort us to cover them with gifts.*

Q: Why do we sing the Alleluia?

A: *We sing for singing's sake.*

Q: At what age can we take communion?

A: *A little bit before we have obtained reason.*

Q: What is the spirit of the Church in the imposing of ashes?

A: *To make us remember that we are under the rod of priests from birth until death.*

Q: What is grace?

A: *I would be less embarrassed if you were to ask me: What are the Graces?*

Q: Who does God give his grace to?

A: *To those who have paid for them in advance.*

Q: What is the feast of the Holy Sacrament?

A: *It's the Church's carnival, the time of holy masquerades.*

Q: How do we know that there is a Purgatory?

A: *From those who have an interest in there being one.*

Q: What is the Jubilee?

A: *It's a monitum of the Church for awakening the devotion and especially the generosity of the faithful toward it.*

Q: What must be done not to lose the effect of indulgences?

A: *They must be paid for to the penny.*

Q: What do you mean by reserved cases?

A: *I mean a particular kind of priestly despotism.*

Q: What is excommunication?

A: *It's a big word that doesn't mean much.*

Q: What is a letter of proscription?

A: *Idem.*

Q: What is simony?

A: *It's a vice native to the Church.*

Q: What is the yoke of the Gospel?

A: *It might have been light in the early days, but it has since become so heavy as to be unbearable.*

Q: Why does the Church say its public prayers in a language unknown to the people?

A: *In order to impose itself on them. The people tend to revere all they don't understand.*

Q: Why does the Church use incense?

A: *In order to make drunk those with weak brains and whose sane reason could cause them harm.*

Q: Why and since when is it no longer permitted to offer animal sacrifices to God, as was once the case?

A: *Since and because men are immolated. It is true that in this century the Church has somewhat relaxed its ancient and respectable discipline. Once it immolated men in their lives, their honor, and in their goods. It would be too obvious today to immolate them in their lives. Immolating them in their honor isn't doable. All that is left is to immolate them in their goods, and men think that they are paying a hefty price.*

Q: Do we have to go the Offering, to the parish mass?

A: *Without a doubt, if there is no money, there are no Swiss Guards; no Offering, no mass.*

Q: What is a miracle?

A: *That which has never been seen and will never be seen.*

Q: What is a mystery?

A: *It is the argument of theologians when they have no other.*

Q: What is prophecy?

A: *It's an authority for those who don't have a good memory.*

Q: What is the Bible?

A: *It s a book whose first edition would be prevented in the interest of good morals if by good fortune it could still to be done.*

Q: What are the Gospels?

A: *It's another Divine Book that the Chinese wouldn't have preferred to the juste-milieu of Confucius and the Romans to Cicero's offices or Epictetus's "Enchiridion."*

Q: What is a priest?

A: *Alas, after God it is the being that has or had the most absolute and obscure power. There would be a philosophical and moral treatise to be written about it that would be quite spicy if it was well digested. It would have as its title: "On Valets and Priests."*

Q: What is a pope?

A: *It's a vicar who knows a good deal more than his priest.*

Q: What is the clergy?

A: *It's a body without a head but with long arms and that never cuts its nails.*

Q: What is Holy Rome?

A: *It's a city where we see many statues and few men and where we meet more masks than faces.*

Q: In order to finish canonically, in keeping with the pious axiom, deus est alpha et omega, tell us again what God is?

A: *It is not I who will respond. I will leave that to the great Tertullian: Deus est ens ignotum et creditum. According to that definition, from a Church Father on the capital and fundamental point of religion, we can know what to think of the rest.*

Philosophico-Moral Prayer to God

For the morning and for the evening of every day of the year, from birth until death

You who I have never seen, and who I only know by name; you whose existence is presumed from the harmony of this universe and denied by the disorder of this same universe. You, of whom it is said I am the child, don't hide my father from me. In order to have me embrace virtue, explain to me how is it that in your empire it is so often unhappy? In order to turn me from vice, explain to me why you allow it to go unpunished? Answer me otherwise than through the mouths of your foolish or deceitful priests. I owe you life; did I ask it of you? You gave me reason to guide my way, and even stronger passions so that I would lose it. You gave me the gift of freedom, and you knew I would abuse it. Author of good, are you also the author of evil? Omnipotent and perfect being, shall you remain indifferent to the fate of your weak and imperfect works? Too far above them through your grandeur, your goodness should bring you closer to them. Pure spirit, how can you act on matter? Alas, in a world of which I am a part I encounter nothing but enigmas, and you, you are the first and the most difficult to solve. . . . Until the day you deign to give me the word, what have I to fear from preferring virtue to you?

Epilogue

What deceiver, in giving us the law, was the first
To attach to our eyes the blindfold of faith,
Degraded virtue through a shameful salary,
Made of beneficent man a vile mercenary,
And, showing him in heaven his remunerator,
Dared to propose a prize outside of his heart. . . .

(*Fragment of a moral poem on God*)

Sylvain Maréchal wrote the above text, which he claimed was from the pen of the father of modern atheism, the priest Jean Meslier (1664–1729/1733?). The ideas in it are derived from Meslier's posthumously published *Memoire*.

■ ABOUT MITCHELL ABIDOR

Mitchell Abidor is the principal French translator for the
Marxists Internet Archive. PM Press's collections of his
translations include *Anarchists Never Surrender* by Victor
Serge, *Voices of the Paris Commune*, and *Death to Bourgeois
Society*. His other published translations include *The Great
Anger: Ultra-Revolutionary Writing in France from the Atheist
Priest to the Bonnot Gang*; *Communards: The Paris Commune of
1871 as Told by Those Who Fought for It*; *A Socialist History of
the French Revolution* by Jean Jaurès; and *May Made Me: An
Oral History of the 1968 Uprising in France*.

ABOUT PM PRESS

PM Press was founded at the end of 2007 by a small collection of folks with decades of publishing, media, and organizing experience. PM Press co-conspirators have published and distributed hundreds of books, pamphlets, CDs, and DVDs. Members of PM have founded enduring book fairs, spearheaded victorious tenant organizing campaigns, and worked closely with bookstores, academic conferences, and even rock bands to deliver political and challenging ideas to all walks of life. We're old enough to know what we're doing and young enough to know what's at stake.

We create radical and stimulating fiction and non-fiction books, pamphlets, T-shirts, visual and audio materials to educate, entertain, and inspire you. We aim to distribute these through every available channel with every available technology—whether that means you are seeing anarchist classics at our bookfair stalls; reading our latest vegan cookbook at the café; downloading geeky fiction e-books; or digging new music and timely videos from our website.

PM Press is always on the lookout for talented and skilled volunteers, artists, activists, and writers to work with. If you have a great idea for a project or can contribute in some way, please get in touch.

PM Press
PO Box 23912
Oakland, CA 94623
www.pmpress.org

FRIENDS OF PM PRESS

These are indisputably momentous times—the financial system is melting down globally and the Empire is stumbling. Now more than ever there is a vital need for radical ideas.

In the seven years since its founding—and on a mere shoestring—PM Press has risen to the formidable challenge of publishing and distributing knowledge and entertainment for the struggles ahead. With over 300 releases to date, we have published an impressive and stimulating array of literature, art, music, politics, and culture. Using every available medium, we've succeeded in connecting those hungry for ideas and information to those putting them into practice.

Friends of PM allows you to directly help impact, amplify, and revitalize the discourse and actions of radical writers, filmmakers, and artists. It provides us with a stable foundation from which we can build upon our early successes and provides a much-needed subsidy for the materials that can't necessarily pay their own way. You can help make that happen—and receive every new title automatically delivered to your door once a month—by joining as a Friend of PM Press. And, we'll throw in a free T-shirt when you sign up.

Here are your options:

- **$30 a month** Get all books and pamphlets plus 50% discount on all webstore purchases

- **$40 a month** Get all PM Press releases (including CDs and DVDs) plus 50% discount on all webstore purchases

- **$100 a month** Superstar—Everything plus PM merchandise, free downloads, and 50% discount on all webstore purchases

For those who can't afford $30 or more a month, we're introducing **Sustainer Rates** at $15, $10 and $5. Sustainers get a free PM Press T-shirt and a 50% discount on all purchases from our website.

Your Visa or Mastercard will be billed once a month, until you tell us to stop. Or until our efforts succeed in bringing the revolution around. Or the financial meltdown of Capital makes plastic redundant. Whichever comes first.